BEST GHOST TALES
OF SOUTH CAROLINA

HAUNTED HOUSES, PLANTATIONS, INNS, AND OTHER HISTORIC SITES

BEST GHOST TALES

Terrance Zepke

ILLUSTRATED BY JULIE RABUN

PINEAPPLE PRESS, INC.
SARASOTA, FLORIDA

*I'd like to dedicate this book to all those
who truly appreciate a good ghost story. Or
it is just a good scare?*

Inquiries should be addressed to:

Pineapple Press, Inc.
P.O. Box 3889
Sarasota, Florida 34230
www.pineapplepress.com

Library of Congress Cataloging-in-Publication Data

Zepke, Terrance
    The best ghost tales of South Carolina / by Terrance Zepke.— 1st ed.
        p. cm.
    Includes bibliographical references and index.
    ISBN 1-56164-306-8 (pbk. : alk. paper)
    1. Ghosts—South Carolina. I. Title.

BF1472.U6Z455 2004
133.1'09757—dc22

                                                            2003027865

First Edition
10 9 8 7 6 5 4 3 2 1

Printed in Canada

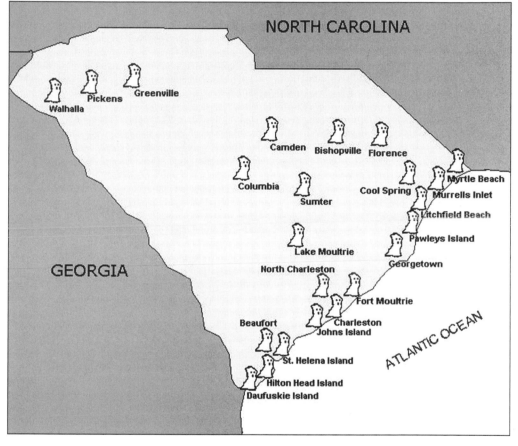

NORTH CAROLINA

Walhalla
Pickens
Greenville

Camden
Bishopville
Florence

Columbia
Sumter
Cool Spring
Myrtle Beach
Murrells Inlet
Litchfield Beach
Pawleys Island

GEORGIA

Lake Moultrie
North Charleston
Georgetown

Beaufort
Fort Moultrie
Charleston
Johns Island

St. Helena Island
Hilton Head Island
Daufuskie Island

ATLANTIC OCEAN

SOUTH CAROLINA

CONTENTS

INTRODUCTION

*D*on't you just love a good ghost story? From the time I was a child to the present day, I have never tired of hearing them. And I like to reciprocate by sharing ones I've discovered. Some of the tales found in this book are well known, some are long-time favorites of mine, and some I just learned while researching this book. I can promise you one thing—these ghosts aren't boring!

Take, for instance, the tale of the Bloodstained Barn. A shiver will run through your body as you read how this barn became saturated with blood. You'll turn the page with anticipation to find out if Lizard Man still roams around deep in Scape Ore Swamp. I'm sure you'll be amused by the ghost who likes an occasional glass of wine. I call him the Cool Spirit at Cool Springs Plantation. And everyone likes to hear about hitchhiking ghosts.

As if these spirits weren't fascinating enough, there is the Hound of Goshen. Many longtime residents of the Lowcountry believe spirits manifest themselves in many different forms, including animals. You'll certainly pause and wonder after reading this tale. Find out what happens when a young woman uses trickery and deceit to get the man she wants in "Betrayal". See if you can solve the mystery of the Land's End Light. Is there a rational explanation or are supernatural forces at work?

The strangest stories surely are "Dwarf Spirit" and "Lowcountry Voodoo". Yes, "Dwarf Spirit" really is about an ornery dwarf who haunts a Beaufort residence. "Lowcountry Voodoo" provides a most incredible look into the beliefs and traditions of Gullahs, who are descendants of West African slaves. I remember one of my great aunts dabbled in black magic, and when I asked my grandmother about it, she told me that voodoo was nothing to mess around with, that powerful evil forces were behind it all. She told me she had seen what could happen and I wouldn't want it happening to me. She made me promise that I would never mess around with it. After that, I was scared to even go near a Ouija board.

What I find most intriguing is that some places are haunted by multiple ghosts. Charleston's Dock Street Theatre has two specters, and so does Battery Carriage House Inn. In fact, one of the inn's ghosts is a torso ghost. He lacks arms, legs, and a head! I've always been curious what kind of interaction these spirits have with each other. Is there any communication or recognition among those that haunt the same place?

The book ends with ghostly definitions, resources, and some tidbits on conducting your own ghost hunt—if you feel brave enough.

No matter whether you're interested in pursuing an investigation of a particular haunted place or just like good ghost stories, I'm sure you'll be entertained by these uncommon spirits.

Well, what are you waiting for? Turn the page and read all about the Headless Sentry who died during an ambush and came back to haunt. . . .

From ghoulies and ghosties and long-leggety beasties

And things that go bump in the night, Good Lord, deliver us!

—Cornish prayer

THE HEADLESS

SENTRY

The renegade leader remained still for a full two minutes, listening for extraordinary noises. When he heard none, Marion extended his hand behind the tombstone. . . .

*F*rances "Swamp Fox" Marion had been in many difficult and downright dangerous situations, most especially after he became leader of the Patriots during the American Revolution. His exploits were nearly legendary.

However, he had trouble getting his body to recognize the persistent commands his brain was sending it. Calm down! He told himself. Despite his best efforts, his pulse was racing wildly and his heart was beating fast and furious. He was experiencing the adrenaline rush that always accompanied these covert missions.

General Marion rode his steed as far as he dared before pulling up sharply on the reins, signaling the animal to stop.

While the horse was adhering to the command, Marion slid sound-lessly down and quickly tied the animal to a tree. He then made his way to the graveyard beside Georgetown's Prince George Winyah Episcopal Church.

As if a solitary, late night visit to a cemetery weren't reason enough for a heart to beat erratically, certainly his current mission was sufficient reason. Many lives were at stake, including his own. The moonlight showed him the way to the tombstone he was searching for, and he dropped to the ground upon reaching it. The renegade leader remained still for a full two minutes, listening for extraordinary noises. When he heard none, Marion extended his hand behind the tombstone, which was inscribed:

LYDIA
Her youthful feet trod flowers that
bloom in beauty o'er her early tomb.

He pulled out a note that had been secured with a loose brick. Marion quickly hid the folded paper in his left boot and left the graveyard as stealthily as he had entered it. Once safely back at camp, he pulled the note from deep inside his boot and thoughtful-ly read:

My dear Patriot,

I trust you received my last communication in due time and that you desire to rescue the prisoner held in our house. In good truth, I perceive that no more appropriate time will present itself for you to free the prisoner than on Thursday next; we will attend a reception at Mansfield Plantation, in the evening. I must warn you that my father, whom I love although his loyalties remain with England, will leave a sentry on the verandah. From your reputation as a leader of your company of men, I rather expect the sentry will cause but little opposition for you. It is not worth my while to try to describe your means of retrieving this man who is being held, for I have not the language to do justice, and I am very much hurried now as I expect to send my letter by Mr. Delavillete, who is waiting for me to write.

Adieu.

Your friend in the name of succès d'estime in the disputes between Great Britain and her colonies.

Hallelujah! The female spy had promised to help him save one of his captured men, and it appeared she was going to make good on her promise.

On Thursday, Marion and several of his men rode into Wedgefield Plantation. The sentry greeted them with a "Who goes there?" His question hung in the air as one of the men quickly unsheathed a sword and beheaded the sentry. His head was still rolling down the plantation house steps as the group entered the dwelling to retrieve their comrade.

A few weeks later, a headless ghost was seen on the grounds of Wedgefield Plantation. It has been seen numerous times over the years in the garden area and is popularly believed to be the spirit of the headless sentry, who was buried here.

The original Wedgefield Plantation was destroyed in the 1930s, but another house was built on the site, which is currently a residential community and Wedgefield Country Club and Golf Course (semi-private). The headless sentry is still spotted occasionally. The house has been made into a restaurant, which is open to the public.

From the Myrtle Beach area, take Hwy. 17 South towards Georgetown. The former rice plantation is five miles north of Georgetown, off 701. Follow the signs to Wedgefield Country Club and Golf Course.

 Francis Marion (1732-1795) served in the state and federal forces during the American Revolution (1775–1783). He was appointed colonel in the Continental Army and a Brigadier General in the militia. He trained troops and performed garrison duty until 1780. He and his men were notorious for upsetting British supply lines and surprising their adversaries.

General Marion earned his nickname "Swamp Fox" because he was highly competent with his war strategies and moved undetected through the Lowcountry like a swamp fox. Marion once returned from an unsuccessful attack on the British near Georgetown. The exhausted officer knocked on the door of Hampton Plantation and asked Mrs. Daniel Horry if he could rest for a bit before catching up to his men, who had crossed Wambaw Creek and escaped to Santee Swamp. The sympathizer invited him in and fixed him supper while he dozed. As she prepared to wake General Marion, she saw British troops approaching. Quickly, she woke Marion and led him to the back door. Jerking it open, she whispered him instructions to follow the garden path to the creek at its foot and then swim to the island that lay opposite it. Once again, the Swamp Fox eluded capture by Colonel Tarleton and his men by hiding in the marsh until daybreak.

It was a long, low gut-wrenching moan the likes of which he had never heard.

It was well after midnight when dispatch got the call, and some of the guys had a good card game going, so McAllister figured that was why no one was anxious to pick up the fare. "I got it," he announced as he grabbed the address from Dick Curton, the dispatcher.

It was a cold, dark night and Bill McAllister couldn't help but shiver a little as he headed to Bramlett Road. By the time he got to the area where the old slaughter yards used to be, the cabbie couldn't shake his apprehension. McAllister pulled over in front of one of the small, brick houses and flicked his headlights. He got out of the car and rubbed his hands together before turning around to face the house.

It was dark and there didn't appear to be any sign of life.

While he was contemplating whether to head up the walkway and knock on the door, he heard a moan. It was a long, low, gut-wrenching moan, the likes of which he had never heard. He swung around searching for the source of the noise because surely some-one was in terrible pain. But he saw no one. The moaning got loud-er with every passing second. It was almost deafening by the time he heard the tortured voice shriek, "It wasn't me! It wasn't me!"

McAllister's grip on the car door handle slipped a few times in his haste to open it, and he fumbled for nearly a minute before suc-cessfully yanking the door open far enough to jump in. As he was starting the engine, he looked up to see a frightening sight that was beyond belief and description. He swerved around the figure, hear-ing all kinds of horrible sounds as he drove off as fast as the car would accelerate.

Trembling from head to toe for the length of the ride, McAllister made his way back to the cab office. He took a few deep breaths, attempting to compose himself. A hand clamped down over his left shoulder and the cabbie nearly jumped out of his skin. "Are you okay, Bill?" Curton asked with a concerned look on his face. "Don't tell me you had an encounter with the Jailhouse Specter?"

"I don't know what it was but I ain't never going back to that area after dark again!" The terrified cab driver related the events to the dispatcher. "I know it don't sound right but I swear on my life I'm telling the God's honest truth!"

"It's all right. I believe you, Bill, because you aren't one to lie and you aren't the first to share this tale. I'll tell you what I know and maybe that'll help you understand things better." Curton took a long drag on his cigarette and a swig of his coffee before continu-ing with the incredible story. "One of our cab drivers, a fellow by the name of Johnny Worthington, picked up a man in 1944. The fare was a black man and that's where the trouble started.

"Johnny didn't like men of color and so made lots of remarks he shouldn't have to this man. It was hard for Johnny to tell if his bigotry was bothering the passenger because the man ignored him. Johnny's wisecracks got even more demeaning as he persisted in trying to get some response from the gentleman. When he pulled over to the drop-off address, the passenger got out of the car and walked off. Johnny jerked the car door open and yelled to him that he still hadn't been paid. The black man turned around long enough to yell back that he wasn't ever going to pay him and he should be thankful he didn't beat the daylights out of him. Johnny ducked into the car and pulled a gun out from under the seat and shot him three times in the back. Next day Johnny told me the story, even sounded like he was bragging. Sure enough, I read in the newspaper that a black man had been found out on Laurens Road, shot dead three times in the back!"

Curton put out his cigarette butt and took another couple of sips of coffee before resuming his story. "This got all kinds of folks more than a little upset. There was lots of bad talk and high emotions for a long time. And then that poor Willie Earle came to Liberty to see his mother. The kid got off the Greyhound Bus and walked over to Reid's Restaurant, where she worked. His mother was so happy to see her oldest son. The next morning, she fixed a huge breakfast in honor of his visit. When she left for work, the twenty-three-year old was hanging out in the living room with a couple of friends. Two policemen came to the restaurant that afternoon, bringing bad news. They told her they had arrested Willie for robbing and stabbing a Greenville area cab driver.

"'Nooo. Not my boy. He wouldn't, couldn't do such a thing. Besides, he arrived by bus. He didn't take no cab,' Tessie Earle reasoned.

" 'Sheriff Maulden arrested him after we took your son by the hospital and the cab driver came to long enough to identify him as the one who did it.'

"No one ever had a chance to find out if Willie Earle actually committed the crime. The police arrested him at his mother's house. The youth was very average-looking—medium build, muscular, no distinguishing marks. While Willie was awaiting trial in the Pickens Jail, some cab drivers assembled at the Rainbow Cafe. The more the men drank, the madder they got. That night they decided vigilante justice was the best course.

"The men led a procession of cabs into Pickens. They arrived at the jailhouse in the wee hours of the morning on February 17, 1947. The pounding on the door brought the jailer, Ed Gilstrap. When he told them he couldn't hand over the prisoner to them, one of the men raised a shotgun and aimed it at Gilstrap's head. The reluctant jailer let the angry mob inside and back to the cells.

"Despite the young man's protests, they took him out to the old slaughter yard (Saluda dam area) and did unspeakable things to him before one of the men, I don't know if it was Hurd or Worthington, shot Earle in the head twice. Johnny was the only one who came back in to work for a couple of hours that morning. He acted like nothing had happened!"

Thirty-one men were charged with Willie Earle's murder on February 21, 1947, but were acquitted on May 21 by a jury of their peers. One of the accused cab drivers later told his wife that he saw the ghost of that boy late one night when he was sent on a call to Bramlett Road. Mae never repeated what he had told her until her husband was deceased. Over the years, many others have reported seeing a ghost in that area. The old Pickens Jail is now the Pickens County Museum.

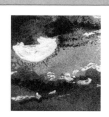 The Pickens County Museum of Art and History is housed in the old Pickens County Jail. The museum has two floors of exhibits, including antiques, historical photos, and art. The facility offers both temporary and permanent exhibits and is open to the public year round. Pickens is located in the north-west part of the state, between Greer and Easley. It is due south of the North Carolina state line, eighteen miles off I-85. 864-898-5963. www.co.pickens.sc.us/culturalcommission/

BLOODSTAINED

BARN

Before another plan could be made, Civil War broke out and the family loaded their most prized possessions and left by boat.

*D*uring the era of slavery and rice plantations, Brookgreen Plantation was one of the biggest in the Georgetown area. Its owners, Josh and Bess Ward, relied heavily on slaves, and their overseer, Fraser, to keep things running smoothly and efficiently. Sadly, Fraser was an extremely cruel man, who seemed to take great pleasure in punishing slaves. He took them into the barn, where he tied them down and lashed them when he felt the men and women had done something wrong or simply hadn't completed a task as quickly as he thought it should have been done. The overseer was always extreme in his discipline.

Once, a slave was caught pilfering some rice. The slave had been stealing a small quantity and selling it in Georgetown in order to buy necessities and liquor. Not only did Fraser whip the man when he discovered the deception, he also found an excuse to punish the slave's wife, and he refused to give the family their weekly rations. Instead, the maniacal supervisor threw an old whiskey bottle into the man's outstretched hands.

During weekly prayer meetings, the slaves discussed what could be done about the problem. All the slaves had experienced the man's brutal wrath and everyone agreed something must be done. It was decided that one of the well-liked household slaves should approach the Wards and tell them about Fraser and his torturous punishment. If he needs proof, the others urged the frightened young woman, tell Mr. Ward to go out to his barn and look at the bloodstained floorboards. The family had gone to North Carolina for the summer in order to avoid contracting "the fever." By the time they returned, the appointed slave had lost her nerve. She tried three times, but always backed out.

Before another plan could be made, Civil War broke out and the family loaded their most prized possessions and left by boat. The day word came that the war had ended and the slaves were all free, they knew what they must do. The group searched the area for the tyrannical boss they had once been forced to obey. When they found him, the men and women were going to tie him up and beat him to death—but not in the barn.

None of them could stand to go in there anymore. The floorboards were soiled red from so much bloodshed, even though they had scrubbed with every kind of cleaner they could think of, and had even tried to hide the stains with hay, straw, and blankets. No matter what they did, the stains reappeared and soaked through whatever covered them. It seemed that nothing could conceal the torture that had taken place in that barn.

Their revenge was never extracted because the evil overseer was never found. When Archer Huntington bought the land in 1930, the first thing he did after inspecting the barn was to tear it down.

 Brookgreen Gardens (800-849-1951 or 843-237-4218) opened to the public in 1932 and is currently one of the most visited attractions along the Grand Strand. It contains 550 sculptures, including many of Anne Huntington's sculptures. Across the street is the 2,500-acre Huntington Beach State Park (843-237-4440, www.discoversouthcarolina.com/stateparks). Tours of the Huntingtons' winter home, Atalaya, are given. Atalaya means "tower overlooking the sea." The park and gardens are on Hwy. 17, near Murrells Inlet.

There's a story about Archer Huntington and a table filled with gold. When the millionaire was building his thirty-room dream house, Atalaya, he employed many local men. Since this was during the Depression, everyone was grateful for the work. Joe, one of the men hired by Huntington during the construction, was later given a job ensuring that there was ample firewood and that most of the fireplaces in the home were kept lit. Since Atalaya had twenty-five fireplaces, this was no small feat. It was long rumored that the Huntingtons kept large amounts of cash on hand, but was never proven until one night when Archer Huntington sent for Joe. He asked his employee to stand guard over a table filled with gold coins. The next morning, Huntington came into the room, quickly thanked the man for his diligence, and wheeled the money cart out the door!

L IZARD MAN

Scape Ore Swamp was such a dense, dark, dangerous place that everyone avoided it. Only things meant to be in a swamp could survive in there. . . .

*T*his is almost assuredly the biggest news story ever to have occurred in Brown Town and Bishopville—and it all starts with retired Sheriff Liston Truesdale. Truesdale was a shrewd man. He had trained at the FBI Academy and had been in law enforcement for over thirty years before being elected sheriff. Over the years, the lawman had seen pretty much everything. Or so he thought. However, the case of the "Lizard Man" had him baffled.

Sightings and strange stories were reported to his department by reasonable, respectable citizens. The first encounter was reported by seventeen-year-old Chris Davis. Davis was on his way home from working a shift at a fast food restaurant in Camden. To return home to Bishopville, he had to drive through Black Town and the Scape Ore Swamp. It was between 10 P.M. and 11 P.M. on July 14, 1988, and the boy had all the windows down to enjoy the slight breeze. He was eating a belated dinner, a big, juicy hamburger and french fries, when he nearly lost control of the vehicle. When Davis pulled over and got out of the car, he found the rear tire was flat. He turned up the radio, opened the trunk to secure the necessary tools, and changed the tire. As he was finishing the task, he heard something crashing through the thick, swampy forest. It was a huge, green beast!

The youth jumped in the car and quickly started the engine. He sped all the way home and then jumped out and ran to the safety of his parents' house. His parents weren't sure what to make of Chris's story. He was not prone to telling tall tales and he certainly seemed legitimately scared. It wasn't until several other sightings had been reported that the boy's father brought him in to share his experience with the sheriff.

Here is the statement that Chris Davis gave Sheriff Truesdale: "I looked back and saw something running across the field towards me. It was about twenty-five yards away and I saw red eyes glowing. I ran into the car and as I locked it, the thing grabbed the door handle. I could see him from the neck down—the three big fingers, long black nails, and green rough skin. It was strong and angry. I looked in my mirror and saw a blur of green running. I could see his toes and then he jumped on the roof of my car. I thought I heard a grunt and then I could see his fingers through the front windshield, where they curled around on the roof. I sped up and swerved to shake the creature off." Chris also told the police that the creature was seven feet tall, had red eyes, lizard-like skin and scales.

About four or five years before Chris Davis had his encounter with Lizard Man, a farmer named Doug Kelly saw it. He was deer hunting near Lynes River and saw something that he said was too tall to be a man but too erect to be a bear. Joe E. Moore Jr. remembers hearing about a "wild man" who frequented the ridge along Hwy. 441 from Sumter County to Lee County (at Brown Town). He doesn't believe there is a Lizard Man. Moore thinks it's probably just a large bear.

"I doubt seriously if anything 'chased' Davis' car down that night. I think he saw the bear's eyes reflecting his brake lights as he was closing his trunk, and by the time he had gotten into the car and gotten it started, the bear had climbed on top of it, which park bears are notorious for doing. Everything I observed led me to believe it was probably a black bear in that particular instance."

However, he's not so quick to dismiss Doug Kelly's story or those told by area farmhands. Nor does he dismiss his father's encounter. When Joe. E. Moore Sr. was a kid, he went fishing with some friends and had an encounter with something in the swamps near Cotton Acres. It scared the kids so much that they bolted, leaving the fishing poles and stuff behind.

During the same summer that Chris Davis witnessed Lizard Man, George Holloman Jr. was riding his bike late one night on the outskirts of town when he stopped to enjoy a drink of water and a cigarette. While he was sitting there, he noticed a tree that seemed to move. When a passing car's headlights illuminated the area, it revealed that the tree had eyes and they were looking at Holloman! He jumped on his bike and pedaled off as fast as he possible. He, too, was reluctant to reveal the strange escapade. It was two weeks after the fact before he did so. A highly respected army colonel, who was also a good friend of the sheriff's, told him about an eerie run-in he'd had, but apologetically explained that he couldn't fill out an official report because it could be damaging to his career.

Late one night a couple was returning from a date when something ran in front of their car crossing the highway. They drove straight to Sheriff Truesdale's office and reported it. The couple was sure it wasn't a person, nor was it a bear or any other kind of animal they could think of. Shortly thereafter, another call came in reporting a sighting, along with a disturbing howling sound, in the same area. The sheriff was called in and a quick search party was assembled. At daybreak, the men began trailing tracks they hoped would lead them to what was now commonly called "Lizard Man," for lack of a better name.

The footprints went to the swamp, which made pursuit impossible. Scape Ore Swamp was such a dense, dark, dangerous place that everyone avoided it. Only things meant to be in a swamp could survive in there, folks reasoned. Sometimes, slaves used to "'scape over" this swamp because plantation owners and masters were not likely to pursue them through the difficult swampy terrain. So the swamp became known as Scape Ore Swamp.

Acknowledging he could use some expert assistance, Sheriff Truesdale contacted the State Law Enforcement Division (SLED). SLED promptly arrived with additional manpower, bloodhounds, and special investigative tools. Plaster casts of the footprints were taken. It was determined that no human could have made the prints and they would have been impossible to fake, given the stride, length, and depth. Unfortunately, rain washed out the tracks before investigators could follow them farther.

By this time, people were starting to panic. It didn't help that the local newspaper had interviewed some of the witnesses and the story was picked up by the wire service. Media from all over the United States and around the world either came to the area or invited witnesses and law officers, including Sheriff Truesdale, on their programs. It was after such an appearance that the lawman got a phone call from Dr. Erik Beckjord, Director of the Cryptozoology Museum in Malibu, California. (Cryptozoology is the study of the lore concerning legendary animals in order to evaluate the possibility of their existence.) He had seen Truesdale on *Good Morning America* and was anxious to help. The scientist read the reports, studied evidence, and interviewed key witnesses. His conclusion was the Brown Town's Lizard Man was indeed a Yeti or Bigfoot. Dr. Beckjord's based his decision on many factors:

- Bigfoot is attracted by food and loud noises.
- Bigfoot roams late at night.
- Bigfoot likes swampy areas such as Scape Ore Swamp.
- The green appearance witnesses described could be swamp algae.
- Strange howlings typically accompany Bigfoot sightings.
- The footprints found were definitely not made by a human nor identifiable animal.
- The car damage was consistent with previous encounters. (For example, Bigfoot damaged the top of a vehicle and then tore an antenna off a car in Washington State, and the chewed up antenna was later found with tooth marks measuring 77 millimeters wide.)
- Eyewitness descriptions

Strangely, the sightings stopped and Lizard Man ceased being a hot topic until July 24, 1990. Bertha Blythers had brought her children to visit her mother in Brown Town. The family went to a local fast food restaurant to eat. Leftovers had been wrapped up and the large, white bag was in the front seat. The group was driving through Brown Town and Scape Ore Swamp, when a large, brown, hairy thing jumped out onto the highway and quickly came around to the passenger side as the frightened woman hit the brakes.

The windows were all down and whatever it was nearly reached in and grabbed her son. Blythers punched the gas and pulled her eleven-year-old daughter closer. Also in the car were her five-year-old daughter, fourteen-year-old twin boys, and eighteen-year-old son. The sheriff was certain this was no prank because people in the area were known to "shoot first and ask questions later" so he didn't think anyone would be foolish enough to pull such a risky joke.

In 1991, a sighting was reported in Richland County. It could have been Lizard Man because there is a huge swampy area near Columbia that is fed by the Congaree River. Yeti or Bigfoot sightings have been recorded worldwide, leaving one to speculate: Where did these strange creatures come from? How many are there? Most importantly, when and where will they next appear?

 Another mysterious creature is Bigfoot. According to Bigfoot Internet Library's website, creatures commonly referred to as Bigfoot, Sasquatch, Swamp Apes, or Skunk Apes, exist in wild and remote parts of North America. Some scientists feel that Bigfoot is not a "missing link" but is most probably descended from the Giant Ape *Gigantopithecus blacki* that was native to Asia and thought to be extinct 500,000 years ago. Others believe that Bigfoot could be descended from *Homo Erectus* or *Homo Sapiens* (human beings), having evolved into a giant form. Some think Bigfoot is an unidentified Hominid (resembling a human being), *Homo gigantus*. The website founder, George Karras, believes that Bigfoot is not human but is closer to human than any animal alive today.

COOL SPRINGS PLANTATION

I jumped up and hurried down the hall to investigate. The guest followed me and pointed in the direction he had last seen the man. . . .

"*D*id you remember to set out the wine glass for Dixie?" John Bonner called out to his friend.

"How could I forget our resident ghost?" Gaffney Blalock quipped.

"Did you say 'ghost'?" asked one of their guests who had arrived early to see if he could help the gentlemen get ready for their party.

"Don't tell me you are unfamiliar with this tale?" Gaffney asked with a twinkle in his eye. "It started when John and I bought Cool Springs a few years ago. The thirty-room, three-story house was built by William and Mary Chesnutt Boykin during the 1800s. Of course, when we saw it, the home was in disrepair, so one had to imagine the grandeur it once possessed."

It was easy to see why John Bonner, the former Curator of Rare Books for the University of Georgia, would find the old homestead so appealing. His good friend, Gaffney Blalock, had taught diagnostic medicine at Clemson University. Restoring the historic home to its original state while adding some modern conveniences seemed a worthwhile task.

John recounts his first encounter with the ghost: "When we finished the difficult renovations, we had a dinner party to show our friends the progress. While we were having dinner, one of our guests asked who the man was he had seen going down the hallway in the opposite direction of the dining room. When I pressed him for more information, he said the man was wearing a blazer and ascot, but they looked like clothing belonging to a bygone era. I jumped up and hurried down the hall to investigate. The guest followed me and pointed in the direction he had last seen the man, who had been heading toward the study. There was no one in the room but a table lamp was on and music was playing. As we surveyed the room, the lively music abruptly stopped and changed to an old-fashioned melody. I went over to the stereo to turn the machine off but it stopped playing the tune just before I reached it."

John Bonner reached down to turn the stereo off only to discover it was already off! He couldn't make sense of it, nor of the strange feeling he had been having the last couple of minutes, as if he had stepped back from the 1980s to the 1880s. The eerie sensation eroded almost as soon as he left the room. A quick search of the house and porch reveled nothing, except that the glass of white wine Dr. Bonner had put down on the porch when he greeted a guest was empty. No one admitted drinking the wine and there was no reason for anyone to lie about the matter.

"The next day I contacted a friend of mine and explained the strange evening, including a description of our mysterious guest. He said it sounded like Dixie Boykin, a former owner of Cool Springs. Mr. Boykin suffered a heart attack in the presence of his daughter. She was on her way upstairs to get his medication when she ran into her stepmother.

"Hysterically, the girl related what had happened and explained her mission. The woman told her stepdaughter that she was too distraught to be of much help and that she would take care of her husband. She sent the girl to her room. Lois Boykin did as she was told. It was another ten or twenty minutes before she heard her stepmother exclaim that her husband was dead. Both his son and daughter swore the woman killed their father. It was never proven that she gave him the medicine. The stepmother forbade them to attend the funeral. Some say the woman could never have done such a thing. Still others reminded folks this was her third husband who suffered an accidental death. Anyway, I'm told the old boy really enjoyed parties.

"Now that we know the history, we're not apprehensive at all. In fact, we always make sure to set out a glass of white wine so that our guest knows he is welcome!"

During this tribute, Union soldier Daniel Hough's gun misfired, resulting in his death. He was buried at the fort later that day, just before the last of the Union troops were evacuated.

*F*ort Sumter, named after a South Carolina Revolutionary War hero, was designed as part of a defense system for Charleston Harbor. Constructed in 1829, the fortification is located on a manmade island of seashells and granite. It stands fifty feet high and the walls are eight to twelve feet thick.

Controlling this military fortification was critical because whoever held it stood a very good chance of winning the Civil War. When South Carolina seceded from the Union, Fort Sumter was occupied by Union troops. The Confederates knew this had to change if they had any hope of winning the war, so they began their campaign to seize Fort Sumter. Union Major Robert Anderson knew this would be their intent and had dispatched several pleas to his superiors summoning support. For whatever reason, President Abraham Lincoln did not take Anderson's warnings seriously and ignored the commander's strong suggestions for additional manpower and munitions. However, he was ordered to continue to hold the fort without engaging in battle.

Meanwhile, Confederate commanders informed him he had one last chance to surrender or the blood of his men would be his sole burden. That night, Major Anderson put his men in the fort's bomb shelters and prayed that Captain Gus Fox would arrive as scheduled with more gunpowder and other important rations. Fox never made it because General Beauregard launched the first attack of the Civil War on the military installation just hours later on April 12, 1861.

It was a huge offensive and the Federals were fired on by Confederates, strategically positioned on every area island. Major Anderson was not able to retaliate because his commanders had not given prior approval to engage in a counterattack. Union troops had no choice but to endure the brutal assault. After almost thirty-five hours of bombardment, Major Robert Anderson conceded defeat with the condition that he be allowed to assert one last command before relinquishing the fort. Giddy over the victory and seeing no harm in obliging, the Confederates permitted a hundred-gun salute to the Union flag before it was replaced by a Rebel flag. During this tribute, Union soldier Daniel Hough's gun misfired, resulting in his death. He was buried at the fort later that day, just before the last of the Union troops were evacuated.

Since that time, some visitors to Fort Sumter have seen the ghost of a Confederate soldier, widely believed to be Private Daniel Hough. A few claim to have seen gun smoke and smelled gunpowder wafting through the air. But I think the most bizarre thing is what happened to the Union flag that Hough had been saluting when he was killed. Not long after this battle, the flag faded just right of the center star, leaving a white spot. A man's face can be seen in this spot. He is wearing a Union hat and his attributes strongly resemble Private Hough's.

If you don't believe me, see for yourself. The retired flag is on display at the Fort Sumter Museum. The site was declared a national monument in 1948. 843-883-3123. www.nps.gov/fosu

THE GRAY LADY

Nina Beaumont begged her fiancé not to go. She struggled to explain what she had seen the night before and her terrible premonition.

I'm sure most locals and enthusiasts of good ghost tales have heard the story of the Gray Man of Pawleys Island. I call him the "Man in the Gray Suit" in my book, *Ghosts of the Carolina Coasts* because it is his suit that is gray, not the man himself! He appears before severe storms to warn of impending danger. Legend has it that no harm will come to those who see him and heed the warning. However, I had not heard of the Gray Lady until a woman shared the story with me during a book signing for the aforementioned book. Here's the story I assembled, after further research.

It begins in France, a few hundred years ago, when a lovely, young woman named Eloise DeSaurin (some accounts have the name DeSaussure) fell madly in love. Unfortunately, her father informed Eloise that her betrothed was not a suitable life partner because he did not share the same religious beliefs. The DeSaurins were devout Catholics, while her suitor was a Protestant. Darce DeSaurin forbade his daughter to have any further involvement with the young man. But love conquers all, or so the stubborn girl believed. She stood up to her father and told him she planned to marry her true love.

Her father retaliated by threatening the lad with strong language and a sharp knife. To further ensure the union never occurred, he sent the defiant daughter to a strict convent. It was so tough that Eloise DeSaurin died less than fourteen months later. Or maybe her untimely death was from a broken heart? Perhaps she had lost all will to live? That's almost assuredly what happened to her mother, who passed away within months of her daughter's premature death.

This was all too much for Darce DeSaurin, who thought he was doing what was best for the family when he sent his little girl to the convent. He had also cut off all contact with his two sons, Raoul and Jules, for sympathizing with their sister. DeSaurin regarded their behavior as a lack of respect for himself and their religion. After the devastating deaths of his wife and daughter, DeSaurin sent for his sons. He made a remarkable confession—he had seen the ghost of his dead daughter!

The vision had haunted him so much that it led him to take his own life soon after his final visit with Raoul and Jules. Much later, she appeared to her brothers when they were in trouble. She brought monk's robes to aid their escape during the St. Bartholomew's Day massacre of 1572. Jules did not escape persecution but the disguise saved Raoul DeSaurin's life.

DeSaurin descendants ended up in Camden, South Carolina. The family home was called "Lausanne," and it was here that Raoul DeSaurin, so named after his brave forefather, brought his fiancée, Nina Beaumont, and friends. During the stay, the story of the specter was reluctantly told by Raoul. Through the years, Eloise has appeared prior to a DeSaurin tragedy. She is always wearing a sad expression and the gray habit from the convent. It sent a quick chill through Nina, but she dismissed the bad feeling as the evening wore on.

However, it came back late that night as she prepared for bed. Nina was so disturbed by the nagging bad feeling that she went down the hall to talk to Raoul's sister, Lucia. As she cautiously walked down the hall towards Lucia's room, she saw a girl clad in gray. Nina Beaument nearly dropped her candle when she got a better look at the figure. It was Eloise DeSaurin! She recognized her from a family portrait that hung downstairs. The girl appeared to be very upset. After nearly a minute or so, the ghostly figure vanished. Nina hurried back to her room, closed the door firmly, and got into bed. She never did get to sleep.

She got dressed very early and went downstairs. The men were already gathered, finishing their breakfast and preparing to leave for a day of hunting. Nina Beaumont begged her fiancé not to go. She struggled to explain what she had seen the night before and of her terrible premonition. The men laughed and made joking remarks. Raoul DeSaurin pulled the distraught woman aside and assured her he would be back in a few hours. There was nothing to worry about, he promised. And with a gentle kiss on her forehead, he was gone. When the hunting party returned, Nina ran out to meet them. What she saw confirmed her worst fears.

Tethered to his horse was the crumpled body of Raoul DeSaurin, who had been accidentally and fatally shot by another hunter. This story was found in a family journal that was discovered after the DeSaurins sold Lausanne. It has come to be understood over the years that the Gray Lady only appears to warn of impending danger.

The house was eventually sold to Mrs. Roger Griswold Perkins in 1884. She converted the large home into an inn, The Court Inn. Guests sometimes confessed to Gray Lady sightings. The Kersaw

County Historical Society tried to save the old dwelling from destruction in 1964, but were unsuccessful in their efforts. It was razed to make way for a residential development. The Gray Lady hasn't been seen since the inn was destroyed.

As I mentioned, there is also a Gray Man. I've heard a couple different versions of "The Gray Man" but the one I included in *Ghosts of the Carolina Coasts* is this one:

The carriage was on its way from Pawleys Island to Murrells Inlet. As the young man bounced inside the buggy, he pondered all the events that had led to this day.

He had met the girl more than a year and a half ago and had fallen in love with her instantly. Not more than two months after that his mother had taken ill. Eventually, it was decided all that could be done for her had been attempted. The doctor suggested taking her to Europe, where more sophisticated treatments were available.

The wealthy plantation owner asked his only son to escort his mother on the journey, as it was nearly harvest time and he could not get away. The young man asked his love to wait for him.

"I will be back as soon as possible, and then I want us to become man and wife."

His mother slowly improved and was finally able to travel and return home. During the boat ride home, they excitedly made plans for his future.

The girl had waited for him and quickly said yes to his proposal. Unfortunately, on the day they were to marry, a terrible storm occurred. For the last five days the weather had been the same. The skies remained dark, the ground stayed wet, and the roads were thick with mud from the downpour. The groom had considered postponing the ceremony until the foul weather cleared, but he just couldn't bear the thought of another long night without his true love beside him. He and his bride-to-be had decided to go ahead with the wedding ceremony in spite of the weather.

His thoughts turned to her during the tedious, rough ride. He knew she would be a stunning bride, and he hoped she would be equally pleased at his appearance. He had carefully selected a fashionable gray suit, tailored especially for him.

As the carriage slowly progressed towards the church, the weather conditions worsened. As he looked out the window, the young man hoped his family would be able to make it. They were coming later in the day, with hopes the heavy rain would slacken by then. The father had tried to get his son to go with them, but the groom was too anxious to sit around and wait and had gone ahead in his own carriage.

Suddenly, the carriage slid in the mud towards the edge of the road due to the impact of the wind. As the driver tried to rein in the horses, they careened again. This time the wind and mud were enough to take them off the road. The carriage turned over several times as it plummeted down the big embankment. The impact of the fall killed both the driver and the groom-to-be.

Today, along the roads around Pawleys Island and Murrells Inlet many locals claim to have seen a young man wearing a gray suit. He appears just before a fierce storm or hurricane hits the area to warn people of the approaching danger. It is also said that anyone who sees the man in the gray suit will come to no harm.

LITCHFIELD'S GHOST

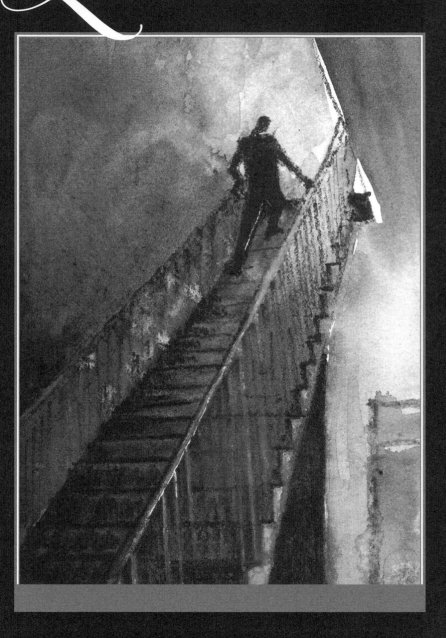

Some guests have reported seeing the benevolent physician on the inn's second floor in a guestroom that was formerly the doc's bedroom.

*L*itchfield Plantation, built in 1750, was one of the best plantation homes in the area. A quarter mile of oak trees lined the entrance to the six-hundred-acre rice plantation. Ideally situated between Myrtle Beach and Georgetown, the house was built by Peter Simons, who was granted the land by the King. Originally, the plantation extended 1,900 acres, from Waccamaw River to the ocean (formerly Magnolia Beach). Simons' two sons, Peter Jr. and John, inherited the property in 1794, dividing it into Willbrook and Litchfield Plantations. Despite many ownership changes, war, and hurricanes, the 250-year-old house still exists. So do the ancient oaks, now affectionately dubbed Avenue of Oaks, which beautifully accentuate the former plantation. Visitors can't help but be impressed by this charming Lowcountry estate.

Perhaps that is why a former Litchfield Plantation owner is reluctant to leave—even many, many years after his death. When

Dr. Henry Tucker resided here, the property was secured by a heavy, wooden gate. It was kept closed and locked after dusk, guarded by a gatekeeper. The doctor often had to make evening house calls. Upon his return, the gatekeeper let him in. However, the gatekeeper sometimes fell asleep, or slipped away to get coffee or food. When this occurred, the doctor was forced to ring the bell many times until the sentry woke up or returned from his personal errand.

Subsequent residents of Litchfield have been awakened by the same sound, even after the old gate was replaced with an iron gate. A few have seen a shadowy figure climbing the backstairs late at night. The witnesses believe it is the old doc because he used these steps when he returned from late night house calls, so as not to awake the sleeping household. However, the ringing bell was the most disruptive event. Whenever it started ringing inexplicably, the noise disturbed everyone in the house. One owner got so aggravated by the late-night bell ringing that he had it removed.

Another former owner, Arthur Lachicotte of Pawleys Island Hammocks Shop, said he never heard bells. But he did sometimes hear footsteps in the old house, which he used for an office. He often thought someone had come to call when in fact no one was there.

Litchfield Plantation is located just north of Pawley's Island, just off Hwy. 17. The former plantation, fifteen miles north of Georgetown and thirty miles south of Myrtle Beach, is now a luxurious resort complete with guestrooms and suites. Additionally, it offers the Carriage House Club, villas, and a Guest House, which is a 8,250-square-foot, brick-and-stucco mansion with six guestrooms. Amenities are plentiful: private beach and marina with dockage, pond, pool, tennis courts, walkway, landscaped patio, courtyards, fireplace, grand piano, formal dining room, library, bar, and breakfast area. Each bedroom offers a king-size bed, cable TV, and private bath. The villas have their own fully equipped kitchens, living rooms, and dining rooms. No smoking or pets are permitted. Children over twelve years old are allowed. For more information, call 800-869-1410 or 843-237-9121 or visit www.litchfield-plantation.com.

Some guests have reported seeing the benevolent physician on the inn's second floor in a guestroom that was formerly the doc's bedroom.

D AUFUSKIE ISLAND

GHOST

The footsteps moved across the upstairs and soon sounded like they were descending the stairs.

*T*he Beattys bought and remodeled the old Daufuskie Island Lighthouse. The Beatty family soon discovered their new home was inhabited by a ghost. The first encounter was experienced by the oldest of the three children, twelve-year-old Nick Beatty. When their parents had to go to the mainland to attend to business or buy provisions, Nick, Jessica, and Rusty were left in the care of a family friend, Sal. Sometimes Jessica and Rusty accompanied their parents, but Nick liked staying on the island and being entertained by Sal. The Italian immigrant was fun to play with and told intriguing stories of his homeland.

On one cold afternoon, the pair stayed indoors and Sal read the newspaper while Nick relaxed in front of the fire. They sat in comfortable silence for a while until Nick saw something he couldn't believe. He watched the living room rocking chair start rocking, as if someone were sitting in it! By the time Sal looked out from behind the newspaper to hear what the boy was stammering about, the rocking had stopped abruptly.

Another time, both Sal and Nick heard footsteps overhead. No one else was home, they each thought as they wondered what was going on. The footsteps moved across the floor and soon sounded like they were descending the stairs. They continued hearing the sound of someone approaching but no one ever appeared. The man and boy listened in amazement as the footsteps crossed the living room. Soon, the rocker started moving, as if someone were sitting in it rocking.

The boy also told his parents he had a friend named Arthur, who told him Daufuskie Island stories. When questioned about where he met this friend, Nick told his parents that the old man came to see him when he was playing by himself. Some swear this is the ghost of Arthur Burns, the former lighthouse keeper who had lived in the dwelling for more than forty years. Burns had to leave the island for a while when he was ill. Upon his return, Burns swore he would never again leave his beloved home.

Although Nick was the first to see old Arthur, other family members have also seen him in the house and outside. They have also heard knocking at the door, but no one is ever there when they answer it.

"Daufuskie is a very spiritual place, and it's full of haints," says Joe Yocius. This is especially true of Bloody Point, where the lighthouse was built. Bloody Point is the southern tip of Daufuskie Island, which guards the southernmost approach to South Carolina. It's named for two skirmishes in 1715 when English troops and settlers massacred Yemassee Indian raiding parties, which had canoed from their safe haven in Spanish-controlled Florida to plunder plantations along the South Carolina coast. In a third encounter at Bloody Point in 1728, Yemassee raiders surprised and killed a British garrison at Passage Fort.

Bob and his wife, Mary, bought the former Bloody Point

Lighthouse in 1999, which was once occupied by Arthur "Papy" (pronounced Pappy) Burns.

Burns had lived in the lighthouse for nearly forty years during his tenure as lighthouse keeper from 1913–1926. When the beacon was decommissioned, Burns bought it. He lived in the dwelling until 1966 when health problems mandated he leave the island. He died less than two years later. His wishes to be buried on Daufuskie were honored.

Most folks believe Arthur still keeps vigil here. Joe had heard the same stories. Some folks swore they saw the old man roaming around the house or sitting on the front porch. He told his wife that he was going to spend the first night alone in their new home. Yocius packed a few essentials, including a small bottle of "liquid courage" and spent the night at his residence. Yocius and Burns must have come to an understanding that night because the couple did move into the old lighthouse.

HOUND OF GOSHEN

When he awoke, there was blood on the back of his shirt, bite marks on the shirt, and shallow bite marks pierced his skin.

*H*ave you ever heard of a ghost dog? I certainly hadn't until I learned about the Hound of Goshen. The story begins circa 1850 when a horrible murder coincided with the appearance of a traveling salesman and his companion dog. It seemed logical to the townspeople that this outsider must have committed the unspeakable crime. Assuredly, it made them feel safer to think some drifter was responsible for the malicious murder, rather than one of their own. Although there was no solid evidence against him, the young man was found guilty on the basis of some flimsy circumstantial evidence—namely that no one could vouch for his character and that he had arrived just prior to the murder. His large, white dog watched and howled during the hanging, as if he was completely empathizing with his beloved master. Soon thereafter, the sightings began.

The first to see the ghost dog was a country doctor, George Douglass, in 1855. It happened on Old Buncombe Road, which ran parallel to the modern Interstate 26. Goshen Township was a village along Old Buncombe Road, where the murder and hanging took place. One of William Hardy's slaves was dispatched to Doc Douglass's home late one night when another slave became gravely ill. The slave arrived, fulfilling his errand, but looking all done in and obviously very scared. With great difficulty, the youth related the message he'd been sent to deliver. As the doc gathered his medical supplies and buttoned up his coat, the slave nearly collapsed in the doorway.

Douglass quickly guided him to a chair, wondering if he had caught whatever illness possessed the other slave. The young slave assured him nothing was wrong, "'cept he didn't want to go back down dat road where dat spirit dog roamed." It was well known that slaves were very superstitious and it would have been foolhardy to try to sway his beliefs. Douglass didn't know what the young man had seen, but he was sure there was no such thing as a " spirit dog." Instead, he got the boy out the door by convincing him they couldn't wait until daybreak or his friend could suffer irreversible damage. The dog wasn't seen again that night, but Dr. Douglass did encounter him another night. After that, he held "superstitious beliefs and haints" in higher regard!

Another physician, Dr. Jim Cofield, also swears to have seen the hound on many occasions. In fact, Cofield's dog was often with him when he traveled this road. Whenever the doctor saw the ghost dog, his own dog would disappear into the woods and would not reappear until Cofield passed the stretch of road the ghost dog haunted.

While Dr. Cofield was not afraid of the hound, many others have reported frightening experiences. In 1936, Berry Sanders claimed the ghost dog chased him nearly a mile. His backward glances yielded the young lad a horrifying vision of a large, menacing dog in hot pursuit. Sanders figured the dog meant to harm him if he ever caught up, so he ran like the Devil himself was after him.

The dog nonchalantly turned around and trotted off when Berry reached the safety of his house.

In 1967, Jim Garrett had a similar rendezvous while en route to a friend's house. The only difference was that he stumbled and fell near the Douglass house as he ran away from the dog. The last thing he could recall before passing out was feeling a heavy weight upon his back. When he awoke, there was blood on the back of his shirt, bite marks on the shirt, and shallow bite marks pierced his skin.

During the 1970s, a woman who lived on Old Buncombe Road spotted the ghost dog as it entered her front yard. She was sitting on her front porch, enjoying the evening breeze, until she saw the dog headed full steam towards the porch. The old woman knew she couldn't make it into the house in time. She fainted right then and there from fear. When she awoke, there was no sign of the dog. She never saw it again. However, that may be because she never sat on her front porch again at night!

The five-mile stretch of land where the ghost dog roams is between Maybintor and Goshen Hill. According to www.allaboutghosts.com, the ghost dog has been seen as recently as 1998, but no further information is given.

 Lowcountry Gullahs believe that a ghost animal (in this case a ghost dog) is really a plateye, a very evil entity taking the form of an animal. For more information on Gullah traditions and beliefs, read the mesmerizing story, "Lowcountry Voodoo."

GHOSTS OF

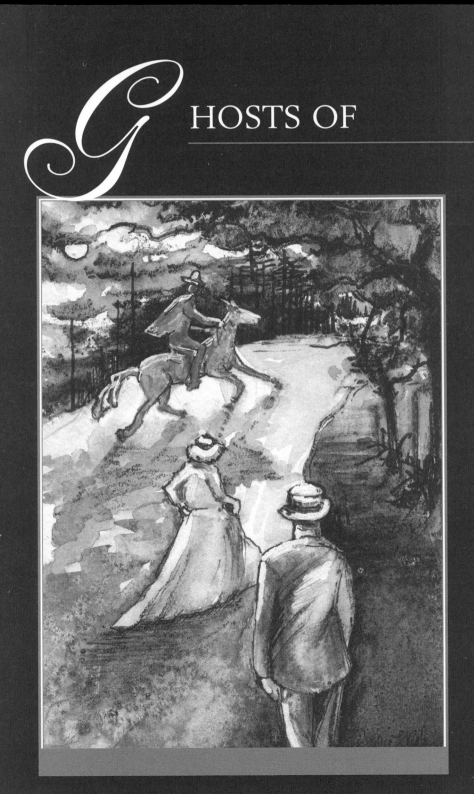

. . . as he sat on the dock watching for a boat full of young people coming from Georgetown, he saw dozens of ghosts.

One of my favorite periodicals is *The Lowcountry Companion*. It is a quarterly magazine filled with unusual information about Georgetown, Pawleys Island, Litchfield Beach, and Murrells Inlet. I had heard stories about the ghosts of Hagley Landing, but it wasn't until I read a story printed in *The Lowcountry Companion* in the summer of 1998 that I learned the specifics.

Eugene LaBruce operated a taxi service, shuttling vacationers and a few locals back and forth from Hagley Landing to Pawleys Island. One evening in 1918 as he sat on the dock watching for a boat full of young people coming from Georgetown, he saw dozens of ghosts.

Believe it or not, that is not the strangest part of this tale. The strangest part was that LaBruce was "transported" to another place and time. He became part of a group of people standing outside a small chapel. Their attire was far different than his own. They were wearing clothing from a period that he guessed was circa 1860. No one seemed to notice him, let alone what he was wearing. Everyone seemed to be waiting expectantly for something. He didn't know what until he saw the couple.

An attractive, dark-haired woman was accompanied by a tall, muscular man. As the crowd closed in on them, almost magically propelling LaBruce forward, a horse and rider galloped up behind the group. All eyes turned to observe the disruption, while a young man dressed in a Confederate uniform urgently pleaded, "Wait! Wait!"

Sadly, he was too late. The love of his life had just committed herself to another man. Worse still, the groom was one of his best childhood friends. The bride grew distraught, realizing the full implications of what she had done. She had waited three years, but it had been a long time since she had received any communication. Naturally, she assumed he had been killed in a battle, as so many of their friends and neighbors had been. The men felt just as terrible. They both insisted the other deserved the girl more.

She couldn't stand to hear them argue over her. The horrible mess was all her fault. If only she had waited a little longer. Shouldn't she have known in her heart that her true love was still alive and that he hadn't abandoned her? But what could she do? Her husband was a good man and she loved him dearly. He had been very good to her. He had offered her much needed comfort and stability, but her heart would never beat wildly for him. She had settled and she knew it. Unable to stand her own thoughts any longer, she ran headlong into the water. The two men followed.

The sounds of an approaching boat caused Eugene LaBruce to look in its direction. As he did so, the church scene disappeared. Gone was the pretty, white chapel, the crowd he had been part of, and the wedding party and soldier. Before he could sort this out in his mind, the bride and groom walked toward him, then right past him up the road, and disappeared. He watched the pair vanish.

The young people had tied up and disembarked by now. LaBruce shook off the disturbing vision and greeted them. He helped load their stuff in his vehicle and proceeded to drive them to the Pawleys Island address he had been given. Out of nowhere, the bride and groom appeared in front of his car. He slammed on the brakes and the young people were thrown forward violently. "What's going on?" they shouted almost simultaneously. LaBruce apologized but offered no explanation. Who would believe me, he thought. After the young people got out of the car, the quiet girl who had sat up front beside Eugene LaBruce leaned in the window and said, "I saw them too!" Then she ran up the walkway and joined her friends inside the house.

You may see them yourself, if you're out on a moonlit night along the road from Hagley Landing on the Waccamaw River to Hwy. 17, just south of the traffic light at Pawleys Island.

PHANTOM

HORSEMAN

General Wade Hampton had a powerful presence during his lifetime, so why not in the afterlife?

Wade Hampton III (1818–1902) held many important government offices, including General in the Confederate Army during the Civil War. He obtained a degree from South Carolina College and returned home to supervise his family's plantations. By the time the war began, Wade Hampton was the richest man in America.

At his own expense, Hampton purchased six cannons for his artillery and four hundred rifles from England for his handpicked men, Hampton Legion Infantry. Before the war was over, Hampton gave all of his own personal fortune to the

Confederates. He was wounded on five different occasions and lost both his brother and youngest son in combat. His oldest son, Wade Hampton IV, was critically wounded. His family home, Hamptons at Millwood, would be burned to the ground by Sherman.

At First Manassas, Colonel Hampton interjected his six-hundred-man Hampton Legion into the conflict, even though they were outmanned, to buy Stonewall Jackson enough time to reach the battlefield. The legion was surrounded, but Hampton held his ground—even after his horse was shot from under him.

On May 23, 1862, he was promoted to Brigadier General and given command of his own Infantry Brigade. When the Confederate Army was reorganized, he accepted Lee's offer to command a brigade in J.E.B. Stuart's Cavalry Division. He was a relentless, courageous, and successful military leader.

When the war ended, he became governor and later senator. He died on April 11, 1902, at the age of eighty-four. Twenty thousand mourners followed his casket to Trinity Churchyard in Columbia. But perhaps this wasn't the end of General Hampton, after all?

In the spring of 1914, just before World War I began, General Hampton was seen in Columbia, South Carolina. Well, sort of. At the intersection of Bull and Blanding Streets, a ghostly sight was observed by many residents. A figure astride a horse was illuminated by a full moon. It appeared to be riding along the treetops!

Those who saw it were terribly frightened, but not because they saw something surreal. People were afraid of the symbolism of the ghost sighting. At first, folks thought it was one of the Four Horsemen of the Apocalypse, a biblical figure foretelling the end of the world. It was much later that someone remarked on the rider's striking resemblance to Wade Hampton. The only logical conclusion was that the dead war hero had returned to warn that another terrible war was about to happen.

To my knowledge, the ghostly horse and rider haven't been seen since that spring of 1914. Perhaps General Hampton felt his duty was fulfilled.

THE DOCK STREET

THEATRE SPECTERS

Somewhere along the way two ghosts took up residence here.

*D*ock Street Theatre was built in 1736. Its first production, *The Recruiting Officer* by George Farhquar, was staged on January 24, 1937. Several good plays and operas were performed over the next few years before the structure, along with many other historic buildings, was lost to a great fire in 1740. Around 1800, a hotel was constructed on the site of the theatre. In 1835, many improvements were made to the Planter's Hotel, including extensive remodeling and the addition of a wrought iron balcony on the Church Street side. This was considered one of the best places to stay in Charleston. Over the next half century, many affluent people stayed here. Like many other edifices, the old hotel fell into a state of disrepair following the Civil War.

In 1838, Nettie Dickerson came to Charleston to make something of herself. She got a good job at St. Philip's Episcopal Church, where the attractive young woman was well liked and respected. One of Nettie's dreams was to marry a successful Charleston businessman, merchant, or planter. The naive girl didn't realize that well-to-do men didn't seek working women from poor families. The twenty-five-year-old was also getting too old, since the prime marrying age in those days was seventeen or eighteen. Furthermore, Nettie didn't have the clothes or upbringing to compete in such a formidable arena.

However, she was often sought after as an escort. When she accepted, it only saddened her to see the lifestyle she so desperately wanted but was unable to achieve. Even her job at the church was no longing rewarding. Within a year and a half of arriving in the port city, Nettie Dickerson was disillusioned and depressed. Seeking a radical change in her lifestyle, she left her position at the church and became a full-time escort. She spent most evenings in the Planter's Hotel, which also served as a brothel until the Civil War.

After several years, Nettie was wealthy but unhappy. Being an escort no longer interested her. To the contrary, she became even more resentful of those who had what she never would. She was happiest when she stood out on the hotel's balcony and surveyed the town from her perch. It was especially exciting when a rainstorm was approaching and the wind blew her long, thick hair in all directions. Sometimes she remained as the rain gently danced on her skin and clothing.

It was one of these evenings that doomed poor, lost Nettie Dickerson. Lightning struck the steel rail she used to support herself as she leaned out into the sky as far as she dared. The electrical current shot through her body, causing her death within seconds.

During the 1920s and 1930s, Charleston residents strongly urged the city government to buy the building and restore the landmark. They decided to return the building to its original purpose. Funds were released from President Roosevelt's Works Progress

Administration and the remodeling was based on London's theatres.

When it was completed, the theatre had several sections—a pit for common people, a gallery for women, and balcony boxes for the wealthy. Local architect Alfred Simons used native cypress trees and wood salvaged from area antebellum mansions for authenticity, however, the theatre equipment was modern and state-of-the-art.

On November 26, 1937, the Dock Street Theatre reopened with a variation of the original Farqhuar play, *The Recruiting Officer*. It was performed by the theater's new resident company, the Footlight Players, and the Charleston Symphony.

Somewhere along the way two ghosts took up residence here. One is believed to be the spirit of Nettie Dickerson and the other the father of John Wilkes Booth. His son fatally shot President Lincoln during a performance at Ford Theatre. Junius Brutus Booth was a member of a theatrical troupe that performed in the theatre. The theatrical troupes were often housed in Planter's Hotel when they came to Charleston to perform at the New Theatre. While staying in the hotel, Booth reportedly tried to kill his manager in 1838.

Nettie's ghost is seen wearing the same fancy red dress with a plunging neckline that she often wore when escorting clients. It was one of her favorite gowns because it was vivid and quite daring, a stark contrast to what was acceptable in the prim Charleston society.

Over the years, many people have had strange experiences in or around the theatre. Her favorite spots are the second floor hallway and balcony. Here are a few encounters I found posted on the Internet:

Jennifer wrote on April 2, 2003: "I was born and raised in Charleston (nineteen years), so my love for the city runs through my veins. I have always been sort of sensitive when it comes to sensing spirits, I guess. I was walking around downtown one day with my mom taking some black and white photos for my collection, and we aimlessly ended up in front of the Dock Street Theatre. I was not paying attention too much, but as we walked by I felt something that caused me to stop dead in my tracks. My mom thought I dropped something and when she asked "what?" I looked to my right and up and there was the balcony and in between the last two windows in the balcony I couldn't see anything, but knew something was there. I told her there is a woman up there, so instinctively I shot a few photos of the balcony. A few days went by and I was in my room (in Goose Creek) when my mom came running in my room ranting about the Travel Channel. I turned to the channel and there was a story about a woman who appears in the Dock Street Theatre. She asked me if I knew about this prior to our trip, I said no, and we immediately bolted to the film shop to develop our pictures. We could have cared less about the other photos at that point, and sure enough, there was the woman! A very slight silhouette of a woman in a period-appropriate dress slightly turned from the street, with details small enough to distinguish her hairstyle. I have shot that same balcony numerous amounts of times at several different angles, and times of day. I have even "asked" her spirit to show herself again, and I have yet to catch her on film again. I guess that just adds to the Charm of Charleston!"

Lisa from Toronto, Canada, wrote on June 21, 2001: ". . . My dad and I were walking past the Dock Street theater at around 11:00 P.M., and if you have ever been to Charleston, there is nobody out late at night. We were walking and talking and it all went quiet and it sounded like someone was walking very fast behind us, almost like they were out of breath. We looked behind, and there was no one there. Just heavy panting for about three seconds. . . ."

That was probably the spirit of Junius Booth, not Nettie

Dickerson. He is not seen but his presence has often been felt. There have also been many strange things over the years involving lights and props that those connected with the theatre simply dismiss as the work of Junius Booth.

Each year, more than six hundred events are performed at the Dock Street Theatre for more than one hundred thousand patrons. The theater is owned and managed by the City of Charleston. The Dock Street Theatre is located in the heart of Charleston's Historic District at 135 Church Street. 843-577-5967.

PIRIT OF MADAME

TALVANDE

Madame Talvande had a high wall built around the school to prevent similar shenanigans from ever happening again.

*T*he Talvande School was the place to send girls from affluent families so that they would receive proper instruction on how to become proper ladies. The headmistress, Madame Talvande, showed the girls how to behave as they were expected.

In 1828, Maria Whaley was enrolled at the Talvande School by her father, Joseph Whaley. The proud father had high hopes for his fifteen-year-old daughter. He believed that she would soon have her choice of eligible suitors—if only he could convince Maria to forget George Morris. Morris had become smitten with Miss Whaley the first time he laid eyes on her cherub face, and nothing her father said or did had altered his affection. Morris was a nice young lad, but Whaley was uncertain of his motives. And even if the boy genuinely loved his daughter, it didn't change the fact that he was not from a prominent family.

The Whaley family lived on Edisto Island at Pine Baron Plantation. When young Morris came to visit, he had no place to stay because Joseph Whaley would not allow him to enter the gates of Pine Baron Plantation. Furthermore, he implored his neighbors to refuse hospitality. The ingenious, love-stricken fellow found a way around this obstacle by setting up camp near the Whaley plantation. And while her father had given express orders that Maria not see George Morris, the two always found a way to spend time together.

In desperation, the frustrated father sent the disobedient child to Madame Talvande's school in Charleston. He figured that with enough time and distance she would forget about the young man. He also figured that it wouldn't hurt to polish her social skills since a proper young lady must know better than to behave so recklessly.

For months, Maria studied and even enjoyed herself somewhat, but she never forgot her true love. The pair devised a devious plan that would ensure they got what they wanted once and for all. On the eve of March 8, 1829, a small group assembled at St. Michael's Church to carry out this plan. Along with the bride and groom, three others gathered for the ceremony. Sarah Seabrook was the bridesmaid and witness; Mrs. Blank, a friend of George Morris' family, smuggled the girls in her carriage, and served as another witness; and Reverend Dalcho performed the ceremony. Maria sneaked out of the school through the back garden and met up with Mrs. Blank and Sarah down the street, where they waited in the carriage.

Due to the late hour, Mrs. Maria Morris was returned to the Talvande School at 39 Legare Street. This, too, was part of the well-conceived plan. Her new husband would come for her the next morning and they would go to Edisto to break the news to her family. George gently kissed his wife goodnight.

Of course, Joseph Whaley was furious when he heard the news. It was some time before he forgave his daughter, but he eventually did and even welcomed his son-in-law into the family.

Madame Talvande had a high wall built around the school to prevent similar shenanigans from ever happening again. The property remained a charm school until 1849. No further scandals occurred, to the relief of the headmistress. The large structure is now a private residence. A ghost has been seen and heard walking the upstairs halls at night. Many believe it is the spirit of Madam Talvande still roaming around, making sure nothing unseemly happens.

$\mathcal{L}$ AND'S END

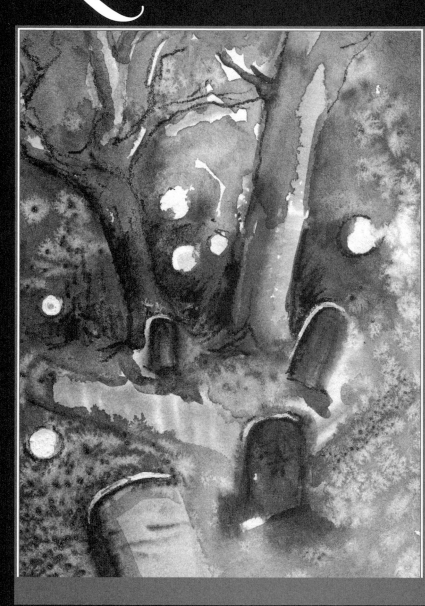

LIGHT

A strange sensation washes over you after you pass under the large oaks and approach the mausoleum.

I know why they call it Land's End Road. When you travel this road, you feel disconnected from the rest of the world. First you pass through Beaufort and then you cross the two-lane drawbridge leading to St. Helena Island. As you cross the island you come to a small community called Frogmore. Watch for a sign for Land's End Road, indicating a right turn off the main road. Proceed to the Chapel of Ease, the ruins of a chapel and mausoleum. This church was built between 1742 and 1747 to serve the planters on St. Helena Island. In 1886, a forest fire destroyed part of this brick and tabby chapel. The ruins and a small graveyard remain.

A strange sensation washes over you after you pass under the large oaks and approach the mausoleum. When you turn the car engine off, the silence becomes most disturbing. Your heart is racing as you open the car door and then try to close it as quietly as possible, without understanding your compulsion to do so. Your eyes will dart in all directions until you get close to the mausoleum. Then you will not be able to take your eyes off the creepy crypt. There is a gaping hole in the front where grave robbers once plundered. The large hole is filled with complete darkness, making the sight all the more frightening.

It is here that many folks, including law enforcement officers and prominent businessmen, have witnessed the inexplicable Land's End Light. The light rises up in the air like a bouncing ball of fire. It lingers long enough to squelch any idea it was just your imagination or a hallucination. Local resident Mary Simpson has seen the light at Chapel of Ease at least a dozen times during her lifetime.

However, another local resident, Lillian Chaplin, says the best place to see the strange light is somewhere between Adam Street Baptist Church and the Hanging Tree, so named because runaway slaves were reportedly hanged from this tree, if caught.

Still others have witnessed the light closer to Fort Fremont, which is at the very end of St. Helena Island. A few months before October 2000, Land's End resident Kelly Brown saw three ghosts in uniform leaning on their rifles around a campfire near Ft. Fremont. Two Beaufort businessmen, Robert Cooler and Deal Poucher, saw it along the road, not far from the fort.

When is the best time to see this mysterious phenomenon? No one can agree on that either. Some say it is only seen on moonless nights. Others swear there must be a full moon. Still others say it makes no difference. There are many who haven't seen it, though not for lack of trying. Approximately a hundred cars could be counted along Land's End Road on any given night about twenty-five years ago, according to the sheriff's department.

I'm told that many years ago, two Marines stationed at nearby Parris Island, saw the light one night and decided to drive through it to find out what would happen. The young men rode right through the bright light and into a big tree. The head-on collision instantly killed one of the Marines.

Scott, a writer for *The Island Clipper*, was working on an article about ghostly sights and tours for their Halloween issue of October 2002. A photographer was dispatched to Chapel of Ease to get images to accompany the story about Land's End Light. He called Scott and told him he thought he should check it out for himself. The photographer told him he felt icy cold and strange. The writer could tell the guy was spooked.

So the next day Scott went to investigate for himself. He also took his camera and shot nearly one hundred photos. When they were developed, he noticed inexplicable balls of light on many of the images. Further research led him to conclude these were ". . . orbs, the most common type of ghost that are photographed. They are commonly believed to be ghosts or colonies of ghost that float in the air."

He returned to the graveyard several times, at different times of night, with his daughter, Crystal. They both had cameras to record images. They felt "cold flashes" one moonless night they visited. When the images were developed, a cluster of orbs showed up just behind Crystal. Some pictures turned out all blue for no reason. "Like I had a blue filter over my lens," says Scott. The second camera stopped working properly. As soon as they got back to the car, the camera worked fine!

The light's origin remains a mystery. Several theories have emerged. The most popular is that the light comes from the lantern of a Confederate soldier who was on patrol during November 1861. A Federal soldier ambushed him and cut off his head with his sword. The head was tossed into Port Royal Sound but the body was left near the road. Many believe the soldier is still looking for his head. Others believe the headless soldier is a Federal soldier who got beheaded during a skirmish. Some believe the light is the spirit of an unhappy slave. The man was sold to another owner and forced to leave his wife behind on the island.

A few believe the light may be the spirit of Private Frank Quigley, from Fort Fremont. He was killed on May 2, 1910, along with five other artillerymen who got into a fight with some local residents. Quigley was the only one who died as a result of his injuries.

Others reckon it's the ghost of a bus driver who crashed into a tree, killing himself as well as his passengers—migrant workers returning home after a long day's work.

In the early 1970s, researchers from Duke University came to St. Helena Island to study the phenomenon firsthand. A participant in the study, Catherine Wooley, published their findings in 1973. She stated that along "ten perfectly straight miles of road," the headlight beams of a car coming on far in the distance would appear to be a single, stationary sphere of light. The researcher credited the abrupt appearance and disappearance of the light to dips and hollows along the length of the road. The light beam would be in motion but the distance gave the illusion of motionless.

Local historian Gerhard Spieler raised two counterpoints to this study. First, the straight stretch of road consists of 2.8 miles, not 10 miles. Secondly, there are no dips or hollows in the road.

Those who have seen the ball of light have tried to come up with a more logical reason for its existence, but so far no one has succeeded.

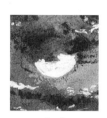 One theory about the ghostly Land's End Light is that it had something to do with a soldier that was once stationed at Fort Fremont. Construction on the fort, which was needed to protect Port Royal Sound from Spanish attacks, began in 1899. However, the Spanish American War was over by the time the fort was finished. Fort Fremont was reportedly the most expensive of all Beaufort area fortifications, but not one shot was ever fired from it! The fort, which is in ruins, is located at Land's End on St. Helena Island. The property is privately owned, so it is not open to visitors.

SS HARVEST

MOON

When the moon is full, an eerie moaning has been heard by area fishermen. . . .

Construction on the USS *Harvest Moon* was completed in 1863. Shortly thereafter, the vessel was bought by the Union Navy for use during the Civil War. The USS *Harvest Moon* was transferred to the Boston Naval Shipyard where she was readied for war. She was the only Union flagship used during the Civil War and she was placed under the command of U.S. Navy Rear Admiral J. A. Dahlgren.

Three months later, the 546-ton steamer ship was sent to South Carolina for blockade duty. The USS *Harvest Moon* patrolled Charleston, Georgetown, and Tybee Island, Georgia. Its job was to keep Confederate ships from getting supplies through to rebel forces. Blockade runners managed to get provisions to Confederate troops, so the USS *Harvest Moon* kept a close watch at these key harbors.

On February 26, 1865, the flagship seized Georgetown's harbor and announced that slavery was over. Next, the vessel was sent to Battery White, which was an important Confederate fort that had just been seized. Its mission was to confirm the status of the fortress, but before the crew could fulfill their duty, Confederate Captain Tom Daggett torpedoed the anchored flagship, causing it to sink.

The following is a report written on March 1, 1865, by Rear Admiral Dahlgren detailing this attack. (Note: spelling is exactly as it appeared in the report.)

Sir:

My latest dispatches had been closed, and not hearing anything from General Sherman at this place, I was on my way to Charleston, but was interrupted for the time by the loss of my flagship, which was sunk by the explosion.

This took place at 7:45 A.M. today and the best information I have now is from my own personal observation. What others may have noticed will be elicited by the court of enquiry which I shall order.

The *Harvest Moon* had been lying near Georgetown until yesterday afternoon, when I dropped down to Battery White two or three miles below, intending to look at the work and leave the next day.

Accordingly, this morning early the Harvest Moon weighed anchor and steamed down the bay. She had not proceeded far when the explosion took place.

It was nearly 8 o'clock and I was waiting breakfast in the cabin, when instantly a loud noise and shock occurred, and the bulkhead separating the cabin from the wardroom was shattered and drive toward me. A variety of articles lying about me were dispersed in different directions.

My first impression was that the boiler had burst, as a report had been made by the engineer the evening before that it needed repair badly. The smell of gunpowder quickly followed and gave the idea that the magazine had exploded.

There was naturally some little confusion, for it was evident that the vessel was sinking, and she was not long in reaching the bottom.

As the whole incident was the work of a moment, very little more can be said than just related. But one life was lost, oweing to the singularly fortunate fact that the action of the torpedo occurred in the open space between the gangways between the ladder to the upper deck and the wardroom which is an open passageway, occupied by no one, where few linger save for a moment.

Had it occurred farther aft or forward the consequences would have been fatal to many.

A large breach is said to have been made in the deck just between the main hatch and the wardroom bulkhead.

It had been reported to me that the channel had been swept, but so much has been said in ridicule of torpedoes that the very little precautions are deemed necessary and if resorted to are probably taken with less care than if due weight were attached to the existence of these mischievous things . . .

I have the honor to be, respectfully, your obedient servant,

J. A. Dahlgren
Rear Admiral, Comg. South
Atlantic Blockading Squadron

Despite his report, there were actually two men aboard ship when it sank—crew member John Hazzard and a young black man. The youth had been a slave at Friendfield Plantation until he was allowed to stowaway by some crew members he had befriended. His family knew their relative had been killed in the explosion but were afraid to let the government know for fear of reprisal. They could very well be charged with conspiracy because they had been aware the lad planned to stowaway on a Federal warship, they reasoned.

Because his spirit was never properly laid to rest, some locals believe he still haunts the shipwreck site. When the moon is full, an eerie moaning has been heard by area fishermen, who tend to be superstitious and respectful of the supernatural, especially as it pertains to the sea. Many still avoid the immediate area around the sunken ship. Part of the shipwreck can still be seen during sightseeing boat tours of Winyah Bay.

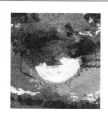 There are as many superstitions involving the sea as there are coastal ghosts. For instance, did you know that thunder, lightning, and fierce winds have been thought to be manifestations of the gods, usually of their anger? If you were struck by lightning, shipwrecked, or drowned at sea, it was because the gods were angry with you. Another sea superstition involves the albatross, which was thought to signify bad wind and foul weather if it circled around a ship in mid-ocean. It was very unlucky to harm an albatross, because it was thought to embody the restless spirit of a dead mariner. Some seaman believed this applied to stormy petrels and seagulls, as well.

HITCHHIKING

GHOSTS

If you've heard many Carolina ghost stories, you probably have already been introduced to the following spirits. You'll note that Lydia, the Vanishing Lady is about a North Carolina ghost. I have included it in this book on South Carolina ghosts because I believe that some stories, such as Swamp Girl, are merely adaptations of the Lydia tale.

LADY IN BLUE

She was a sweet young girl, sixteen years of age. The child's big blue eyes and cherublike face were framed by golden hair. She lived with her father, her mother having passed away during childbirth. He was the sole keeper of Hilton Head Lighthouse, a rather large responsibility. The man was very conscientious, which was reflected by the many citation medals awarded him by the Lighthouse Board.

The channel and sound surrounding the uninhabited island made it a treacherous route for mariners on their way to other

North and South Carolina ports, as well as those passing by Georgia en route to Florida. To keep the light at optimum operating level, he spent his days making sure the lamp's wicks were cleaned and properly trimmed and the lamp and lantern room's windows spotless. Every evening he faithfully hauled buckets of oil from the nearby shed and up the multitude of steps to the lantern room to keep the light burning brilliantly until daybreak.

One night after supper he told his daughter he was going to check the light, just as he did every night. Within minutes, a storm had arrived at the island. The storm gave way to a hurricane, and rain pelted against the glass panes of the watch room and lantern area. Wind accompanied it and circled the tower like an angry force unleashing itself. Thunder and lightning crashed and filled the sky while waves furiously slapped the shore. One of the windows shattered from the force of the gale, causing the lamp to flicker. The keeper covered the hole as best he could, and he then spent hours running up and down the stairs to relight the wick or bring more fuel, until he was out of breath and a deep pain filled his chest.

By this time, his daughter had awakened and was frightened by the fierce storm and the absence of her father. She grabbed a dress out of her closet and put on her coat. As quickly as her feet would carry her she crossed the walkway that led from the house to the beacon. There the girl found her father slumped over a step. Despite her crying and begging, he didn't awaken.

The storm had hit the area hard, and it was a couple of days before anyone came out to the island to check on the family. What they found was a tragic sight. Father and daughter were on the tower steps, both dead. She was wearing a pretty blue dress, and he was clutching a lantern and oil bucket. It was later determined the poor man had suffered a heart attack and the girl had died from shock and trauma.

From that night on, whenever a terrible storm is approaching, a young woman wearing a blue dress has been seen warning others of the impending danger and signaling with her arms and hands to "go back . . . go back . . ."

One couple even claims to have picked up a young, blonde girl wearing a simple blue dress and worn coat soaked from the rain. As the man drove, his wife turned around to talk the girl, but no one was there! The Lady in Blue had vanished into thin air. The woman was so upset that the man had to pull over to comfort her and look for the missing passenger. He never found the girl who had gotten into their car, but the back seat had to wiped down from all the water left by the drenched stranger.

SWAMP GIRL

The sightings have occurred in the Greater Columbia area. There's a swampy area along Hwy. 378 leading from Sumter to Columbia and it is on this stretch of road that the girl makes her appearance. She is outfitted in black from head to toe, from the long black dress to the black hat and black bag. When motorists stop to see if they can be of assistance, she gratefully accepts a ride into town. The upset and tired young lady shares that her mother, who lives on Pickens Street, is very sick and that is why she is so desperate to get to Columbia.

Over the years, many folks have come to her aid, only to have her vanish upon arrival at the Pickens Street address or en route! Whenever the motorist has summoned the courage to leave the vehicle and go up to the house and knock on the front door, he or she has been told by the occupant that the swamp girl was the homeowner's sister. She was killed in a car wreck when the Wateree

95

River Bridge was first built, trying to reach her sick mother. She is seen on the anniversary of her death, I'm told.

I attended the University of South Carolina at Columbia, traveled these highways many times, and even lived on Pickens Street, briefly. However, it wasn't until I started researching and writing ghost tales that I learned about Swamp Girl. At the risk of upsetting any true believers, I must say that I'm inclined to think that this is yet another version of Lydia.

WALHALLA HITCHHIKER

During the 1930s, Larry Stevens owned a small yellow and black plane, which he housed at the Greenville-Spartanburg Airport. Stevens enjoyed the serenity and panoramic views that flying provided. He often went out on aerial sightseeing excursions. Tragically, it was on one of these pleasurable outings that he crashed into the mountains, ending his life instantly. A horrific hail storm developed while he was out that afternoon and his visibility became significantly impaired.

The next day, another pilot spotted the wreckage near Walhalla. This should be the end of a very sad story, but it is just the beginning.

Hwy. 107 adjoins Hwy. 28 near Oconee State Park. This road takes travelers into several South Carolina cities, including Anderson, Clemson, and Walhalla. Ever since this plane crash, a hitchhiker resembling Larry Stevens has been seen along this route. He wears the same attire as the dead pilot—a loose-fitting, well-worn, dark-colored, all-weather coat. Depending on where he is picked up, the wet stranger asks to be let out either at the Piedmont Overlook or Moody Springs. These are odd requests, indeed, considering the hitchhiker is only seen on dark, rainy nights. These conditions would hardly be suitable for visiting a scenic overlook or natural mineral springs!

Former Superintendent Bob Cothran heard many tales about the Walhalla hitchhiker during his tenure at Oconee State Park. Every time the hitchhiker is dropped off, he disappears almost as soon as he is out of the vehicle. Folks like to think it's the spirit of Larry Stevens, still hanging around enjoying his beloved mountains.

LYDIA, THE VANISHING LADY

This must be one of the most widely circulated tales in the state. Many entries in the "Ghost Watch" contest were simply variations of this story. (The "Ghost Watch" contest was held to obtain personal accounts of ghostly encounters. The winning entries were included at the end of my book *The Best Ghost Tales of North Carolina*—see last page of this book). The original story is about a girl named Lydia who had been at a dance in Raleigh with her boyfriend. In the early 1900s, a road was paved that linked Greensboro to High Point. The road ran through Jamestown and a narrow underpass beneath the railroad tracks. The pair was probably discussing what a wonderful evening it had been, perhaps even making future plans, as they drove home to High Point.

It was a dark night and drivers were not paying as much attention as they should. Lydia and her boyfriend collided with another car at the underpass, and Lydia was killed instantly. Ever since that tragic night in 1923, a young lady garbed in a white ball gown has often been spotted on the side of the road waving for help.

Burke Hardison is one of the motorists who claims to have seen the specter. It was very late as he passed through Jamestown. As

Hardison approached the underpass, he saw a girl wearing a light-colored dress. She was frantically signaling for help. Knowing something must be terribly wrong for this lovely young woman to be all dressed up and standing alone on the side of the road at that time of night, he quickly pulled over.

"What's the matter?" Hardison asked with concern. The girl told him she was desperately trying to get home to High Point.

"My mother will be terribly worried," she said softly.

He told her to get in and he would gladly take her home. She said, "thank you," and gave him the address as she got in the vehicle. Lydia leaned wearily back in the seat and offered no more information as she closed her eyes. Although he was dying of curiosity, Hardison didn't ask her any questions.

He knew how to get to the street she had named, so he turned off the highway and continued without saying a word. He glanced over at his passenger and noticed she looked as if she was sleeping. Hardison wondered how long she had been waiting for someone to come by. What was her story? He thought he might find out when they reached their destination, but when he went around to open her door, she was gone. It wasn't possible, but she had vanished!

Determined to get to the bottom of the bizarre occurrence, Hardison marched up to the door and knocked. After a few minutes, a woman answered. Before the odd tale could be told, the sad-looking woman said, "I know why you're here. You're not the first person this has happened to, and you almost assuredly won't be the last."

She explained how her daughter had been killed in a car wreck some years ago. The woman told him that motorists occasionally showed up claiming they had given a girl a ride home but she had disappeared upon arriving at the house.

She seems so tired and troubled that no one ever presses the girl for more information. The few times those who picked her up tried, all they got out of her was that her name was Lydia and that she wanted to get home as soon as possible. With tears welling up in her eyes, the woman told Hardison that she wished someone could bring her daughter home.

I interviewed a Jamestown resident who thinks he saw Lydia when he was a teenager. Years ago, there was a dirt road that extended to the area around the underpass. He was out one rainy night with some other youths on that road when his truck got stuck in the mud. The boys got out to push the vehicle and he saw something white behind him. They didn't stick around to get a better look. They ran off and didn't come back for the car until the next day. I talked to several longtime residents of Jamestown, but no one knows just when Lydia was last seen. I was told the best chance of seeing her was on foggy or rainy nights.

Pranks have occurred due to the folklore surrounding Lydia. High school students have outfitted themselves in fancy white dresses and appeared as cars approached the underpass. But those who say they have picked up Lydia on the side of the road say it is no laughing matter. They are haunted by the image of a beautiful young woman trying to get home but never quite making it.

URDER TIMES TWO

Two men who were in the area fishing heard the shot and watched in horror as the woman's entire body violently shuddered for a few seconds and then toppled to the ground face first.

*D*r. Cleveland Bigham murdered his wife to protect a terrible, dark secret. The Bighams were wealthy and influential citizens of Florence County. The family owned a great deal of farmland and employed many farmhands. Cleveland's brother, Smiley Bigham, had an argument with one of the hired help, a youth named Arthur Davis. The bad-tempered employer hit the lad a couple of times during the course of the disagreement. Arthur Davis cried out in pain and ran off to avoid further assault.

Unfortunately, Smiley brewed about the event for the rest of the day. He worked himself up into a proper rage. Smiley told his family he would not, could not, let the matter drop. He would have his revenge if it was the last thing he did, he vowed. The next day, the mangled, battered body of Arthur Davis was found in the woods, not far from his home. His mother told the sheriff that three men wearing masks had come to her house late the night before. When she refused to let them in, the trio barged into the residence. After a quick, frantic search, they found her son hiding under his bed and dragged him out of the house, despite her pleas to leave the poor boy alone. She adamantly swore that one of the men was Smiley Bigham. "I know his voice. If that weren't enough proof, one of the other men hollered out to Smiley that he'd found the boy. Clear as a bell, he shouted out, 'Smiley, we got him.'"

The sheriff knew he had to tread lightly or risk the wrath of the large and powerful Bigham family. He brought the three men in for questioning but made no arrests. The community was outraged by the murder and demanded justice. The sheriff was forced to arrest Smiley Bigham and his cohorts. The trial was set and the men were released on bond. The close-knit clan pledged their allegiance to Smiley. Everyone agreed to testify that Smiley couldn't have been involved in this crime because he was home all evening on the night in question. There was only one holdout, Ruth Bingham. She knew he'd left the house that night and was certain her brother-in-law had committed the heinous crime and thought he should pay for it. No, she would not take part in this charade, she told the family.

Cleveland assured his brother that Ruth would not betray him or the Bingham family. Smiley remained doubtful that his brother could elicit such a promise from his wife. After all, they'd only been married one year and she didn't seem to have any idea what family loyalty was all about. The strain of the situation was almost unbearable for Ruth Bingham. She had fallen madly in love with Cleveland when she met him. It had been a whirlwind romance. He was strong, smart, handsome, and considerate. Yet, his personality took on a hard edge when he got around his family. She was almost afraid of him when he told her she must give the same testimony as the rest of the family at Smiley's trial. Desperately needing to get away from her husband and his family, Ruth packed a couple of bags and went to her old home in Mountville to stay for a while.

During her long visit, Ruth received dozens of letters and telegrams from her husband insisting she return home. She finally realized she had no choice but to go back to her husband. Despite what had happened, she loved him. Also, she was afraid to defy him any longer. Ruth made arrangements to go back to their residence in Harpers. Upon her return, Cleveland informed her they would leave in a couple of days for Sunnyside. The former plantation home on Murrells Inlet had been made into a fishing lodge by its owners, the Avants.

This vacation was supposed to be a chance for them to patch up their differences, but that never happened. Ruth would not change her mind about Smiley and the trial. He had brutally murdered a young man for no good reason and should be punished for it. It was even more upsetting that her husband didn't think so. No matter what, family sticks together, he told her. The couple was barely speaking and the marriage was in jeopardy. Ruth tried to avoid her husband as much as possible by taking long walks and solitary swims.

One afternoon as she prepared to take a swim, she saw her husband on the porch with William Avant. Ruth slipped on her husband's long gray coat over her swimsuit and exited through the side door of the house so as to avoid detection. Dusk was approaching as Ruth made her way to the water and the men sipped whiskey. As she stood looking out over the water, the young woman began unbuttoning the coat. A gunshot caught her squarely in the back before she could remove the garment. William Avant had shot Ruth Bingham! She fell to the ground and lay there motionless as the full realization of what he had done hit him.

Avant and Bingham rushed to where Ruth lay crumbled on the ground. Two men who were in the area fishing heard the shot and watched in horror as the woman's entire body violently shuddered for a few seconds and then toppled to the ground face first. The two witnesses arrived just as Bingham scooped up his injured wife and carried her to the house. He trotted up the steps and laid her down on the porch of Sunnyside. The doctor leaned over his wife, presumably checking her pulse and breathing. It was a horrifying scene. Ruth Bingham lay in a pool of blood and her husband was covered with blood from carrying her up to the house. He wiped the long wisps of hair from her face and then turned to shake his head to inform the others that she was dead.

Since he was the owner of Sunnyside and the one who was responsible for the tragedy, William Avant insisted on going to get the sheriff and coroner. After examining the body and hearing Avant's story, the coroner proclaimed, "the deceased came to her death by gunshot wounds, by mischance, at the hands of W. B. Avant and G. C. Bingham as accessory thereto; both men laboring under great mental excitement and fear at the time of the deed."

Avant and Bingham told the authorities that they thought the figure in the coat was a burglar and were in fear for their lives. They also said they called out to the figure but received no reply. Sensing imminent danger, Avant grabbed up his rifle and fired. Of course, this was not the truth.

The real story, supposedly, is that the men thought they had seen a ghost. Bingham had Avant convinced that the shadowy figure down near the water was the ghost of Sunnyside. Avant had confided that he believed Sunnyside was haunted. On a couple of occasions he thought he had seen an apparition at the porch window and also down by the water. Avant didn't like the thought of living in a haunted house, not one bit. Cleveland Bingham told the frightened man that there was only one sure way to get rid of a ghost and that was to shoot it. The spirit would realize it was unwelcome and would take its leave, the physician assured Avant.

Avant probably wouldn't have swallowed this tale if not for two things. First, Bingham had spent the better part of the day working on Avant. He had him good and scared by the time they saw the "ghost." Also, Bingham had been pouring generous portions of whiskey for the last two hours, so Avant's physical reactions were a might quicker than his mental reasoning. William Avant soon realized he had been used by his so-called friend, Cleveland Bingham, but figured their stories had better match. It would not be wise to get into finger pointing, especially since he had been the one to shoot Ruth.

Friends and family of Ruth Bingham were quick to point out that this had been a clever ruse by Cleveland Bingham to protect his brother and get out of a bad marriage. It was no secret that the relationship had been deteriorating. Ruth had left her husband and they had reconciled only a few days before her death. They were convinced that he had pleaded with her to come back just so he could carry out his plan to get rid of her. The two men who had been out fishing when they witnessed Ruth's shooting said they couldn't imagine her being mistaken for a ghost or burglar. If they could tell she was a young woman from way over where they were fishing, anybody sitting on the porch could surely see that, as well.

Furthermore, the fishermen were absolutely positive that they didn't hear any shouts before the shots were fired. Avant and Bingham had said they called out to the "burglar" several times to identify himself or be shot. It was thanks to the witness statements and scathing articles that appeared in several major newspapers, including Columbia's *The State*, *Georgetown Times*, and *Charleston News and Courier* that Cleveland Bingham and William Avant were charged with the murder of Ruth Bingham.

Also on trial were Smiley Bingham and his two accomplices for the murder of Arthur Davis. With the Bingham family swearing that Smiley never left the house the night Arthur Davis was murdered, and without Ruth Bingham's testimony to the contrary, the men were found not guilty.

Many feared both brothers would get off scot-free. However, the two fishermen, Mr. Smith of Mullins and Mr. Murchison of Marion, were unwavering in their testimony that it would have been impossible to mistake the young lady for a ghost or burglar. Other witnesses gave statements about the marital trouble and about the pressure the family had put on the deceased to give corroborating testimony at Smiley Bingham's trial. Both men were found guilty and the judge sentenced them to three and a half years.

Bingham's attorney appealed the decision and the South Carolina Supreme Court released Cleveland on a $1,500 bond. By the time an error in the appeals process was realized and bail revoked, it was too late. The Binghams had deeded the bail property over to others. The Bingham family had known Cleveland would forfeit bond because they helped him escape, although that would never be proven. William Avant was also granted bail. By the time the South Carolina Supreme Court found both men guilty they were long gone.

William Avant was found in Texas and extradited to South Carolina, where he served his sentence. After his release, Avant joined his wife and daughter but he didn't live happily ever after. Unable to forget the shooting, he went off for days at a time on drinking binges and often went days without eating a proper meal. He died shortly after getting out of prison. Cleveland Bingham, on the other hand, seemed to have no remorse. He remarried and moved to Atlanta, Georgia. It is even rumored that he came back from time to time and had secret visits with his family.

The ghost of Ruth Bingham began appearing at Sunnyside after the first trial. She has been seen walking along the creek at dusk. No doubt she would like a chance at retribution.

WHOOPING AND

According to a former caretaker, the ghost appears on the front steps of the small house wearing a flowing robe and Cinderella-like slippers.

Strangely enough, when Wampee Plantation was being built, a tornado came through and destroyed everything in its path, except for this dwelling. The plantation's original owner was John Stewart, who received a land grant for 840 acres on the west side of Biggin Swamp in 1696. That same year Baptist minister, Rev. William Screven, and many of his followers, arrived from Maine. A few years later, Rev. Screven bought several hundred acres of land adjoining John Stewart's plantation. Eventually, this all came to be known as Wampee Plantation. The property changed ownership many times over the years and this house is actually the third residence. Many swear it is haunted, but by whom?

According to a February 25, 1865, entry in a diary possessed by Miss Charlotte St. John Ravenel, "The negroes have most terrifying stories this morning; the enemy have marched through Pinopolis and were yelling at Wampee last night, others said they heard great whooping and yelling as if someone were driving a hundred head of cattle."

Clusters of Indian burial mounds have been discovered at Wampee and Ophir Plantations. Several Charleston Museum members conducted an archaeological dig a few years ago and found charred bones (the Indians cremated warriors who died in battle), pottery, arrowheads, and the remains of an Indian sitting in a crouching position. One theory is that these Indians were descendants of the Lost Tribe of Israel or that they somehow ended up at Wampee, arriving from other countries with 55 dialects. The Indian children played ceremonial games and performed dances of the buffalo, crow, and other animals. There was even a scalp dance. Many believe the resident ghost is the spirit of a young woman who was killed after following her mate into battle.

According to a former caretaker, the ghost appears on the front steps of the small house wearing a flowing robe and Cinderella-like slippers. Perhaps the apparition is not a young Indian woman but rather the spirit of one of the former plantation owners, such as Mrs. Sabb or Mrs. MacBeth. Maybe she lingers to make sure her beloved home is being properly cared for.

She has also been seen in many of the dwelling's rooms and vanishes as quickly as she appears. The caretaker cites other extraordinary experiences, such as the time he saw "two white objects moving back and forth" on the front piazza. There were no heads but a "peculiar rattle of feet." The current caretaker, Sandy Gibson, swears, "it's a very friendly ghost." Once he walked down the stairs after turning the lights off downstairs and found they were back on. "Santee Cooper's rates are so low, I decided to leave them on," he said with a chuckle.

The apparition is most often observed on the upstairs landing. "The guard who patrols at night saw a lady standing upstairs," said

Gibson. "Things move around," said Gibson. A guest once found a tie he had placed on the other bed on his bed the next morning. A towel in one bathroom was moved to another bathroom. Myrtle Beach City Council uses the former plantation home as a retreat, but members merely smile when asked if they have had any unusual encounters.

The former plantation is located one mile from Pinopolis, at Lake Moultrie, which is about twenty miles northwest of North Charleston. Lake Moultrie is between Lake Marion and Francis Marion National Forest, off Hwy. 6.

BETRAYAL

To her shock and discernment, he informed her that he would never live under the same roof with her.

*R*uth Lowndes had her mind set on Francis Simmons for quite a while. He was ruggedly handsome, wealthy, and well-liked. So what if her heart didn't beat wildly whenever he was near? So what if she didn't daydream about him? Ruth was far too pragmatic to be concerned that she wasn't in love with Francis. The most important thing was that Ruth had chosen a man she felt best suited her needs. Francis had an excellent reputation for being a perfect gentleman and would take good care of her, she was certain. And, she was attracted to him. That was enough to initiate a long-term partnership. The rest would come in time as they conceived their children and the years passed comfortably.

Ruth probably would have changed her mind and done things differently if she had known the final outcome of her plan.

There would be no children. There would be no lavish parties co-hosted by Ruth and Francis. There would be no real marriage. And Ruth could only blame herself. Who else could she blame for the duplicity that she alone had imposed on Francis Simmons?

It all started with an oyster roast held at the Simmons plantation on Johns Island. Ruth introduced her best friend, Sabina Smith, to Francis at this social. They took to each other instantly and spent much of the day off walking or talking on their own. Ruth was consumed with her own activities and didn't think much about it until later when Francis commented how wonderful Sabina was. Ruth noticed the look in his eyes as he discussed Sabina and how great a day it had been. She realized he had fallen for her best friend. She had to act fast!

Ruth didn't have to wait long for an opportunity. She saw to it that Dick Johnston took Sabina and another friend back to Charleston before Francis could volunteer to do so. She lingered after the other guests had departed, but Francis scarcely seemed aware of her presence. Ruth kept talking, hoping to engage him in conversation, but the young man's thoughts seemed to be somewhere else. He was daydreaming about Sabina, she realized.

"Don't Dick and Sabina make a lovely couple? she blurted out.

"What?" he mumbled trying to be polite but completely uninterested in anything Ruth had to say.

"I said, don't Dick and Sabina look good together?"

"What? Why would you say that?" he asked.

"Dick Johnston and Sabina Smith are betrothed," she announced slyly.

"They are?" he questioned disbelievingly.

"Now Francis Simmons, don't you pretend you didn't notice how happy they are!" Ruth admonished. "They've been seeing each other for some time now and Sabina is simply over the moon about him. That's all she's talked about lately," Ruth rambled on, pretending not to notice the tortured look on his face. "I think they're going to make an official announcement at next month's society ball."

Francis was unable to speak. He could hardly think. The only thing he knew was that the girl he had fallen in love with as soon as he saw her was promised to another. Why hadn't she mentioned it? The way she responded to him, the way she looked at him . . . how could she if she had such feelings for another man? Had she just been toying with him? Flirting for the sake of her own amusement or vanity? He felt sick to his stomach. As he waited for the queasy feeling to subside, Francis wondered why Ruth had shoved a handkerchief in his face. Did she realize how close to illness he felt?

"The embroidery work on this lace handkerchief is really wonderful!" she cried out, hoping to steer his thoughts away from Sabina. Her ploy worked. He took the handkerchief she had thrust upon him and remarked, "Yes, it is indeed beautiful. Don't you wish you had these initials?" he said as he fingered the material, remembering the occasion his sister had given it to him.

Ruth had the biggest smile on her face as she exclaimed, "Yes, yes I do."

The next afternoon Francis was summoned to the Lowndes home. Rawlins Lowndes took the young man into his study and offered him a drink. Once the two men were seated opposite each other, sipping their drinks, the older gentleman revealed his reason for the invitation.

"I think Ruth made an excellent choice," he began. "Although I am surprised that you did not approach me first, I give my full and joyous blessing to the union. I would be honored to call you family. I already think of you as a son," he acknowledged humbly and raised his glass.

As though a load of bricks had dropped on his head, Francis

realized that Mr. Lowndes was under the impression that he had proposed to his daughter! He thought back to the previous day and remembered the brief conversation they had at the end of the party. He recalled they talked about a couple of guests and a handkerchief his sister had made for him. Surely she hadn't misconstrued the conversation about the handkerchief to mean something more. Ruth had seemed very happy, almost giddy, during the ride home. Surely he wasn't about to be trapped into a marriage over something so ridiculous?

When he looked back at the grinning old man who held his glass high to signal a toast, he knew he was trapped. Rawles Lowndes was like a father to Francis. His own father had died when he was just a boy and Rawles had not only helped the Simmons hold on to their plantation, but the rice plantation had flourished under his guidance.

No, he would not bring dishonor to the Lowndes family by negating Ruth's claim. Besides, what did it matter? If he couldn't be with Sabina, it didn't matter who he married. Francis Simmons raised his glass to meet the other. The deal was done. After quickly consuming the drink, Francis and Rawles stood and shook hands. The older gentleman leaned in and gave Francis a big hug. "Ruth couldn't find a better man. Take good care of my girl," he said softly, choked with emotion.

Francis was late to the wedding. On his way to the church, he couldn't help but pass by Sabina's house. He saw her sitting in the garden. Impulsively, the young man raced over to her. Without speaking, he took her hands in his. She was so exquisite, he marveled.

"I want to extend my best wishes on your nuptials. I sincerely hope you will be happy. I hope you understand why I cannot attend," she almost whispered.

"Oh, Sabina, I bestow the same wishes for your marriage," he said reluctantly. He reached and took her in his arms for what he knew would be the first and last time. It felt so right he didn't want to ever let go of her.

"What marriage?" Sabina asked.

"I understand you will soon wed Dock Johnston," Francis stated.

"That's not true! How could I have a future with him, or anyone else, when my heart is no longer mine to give?" she asked.

After searching her face and feeling her warm embrace, he pulled her closer to him and whispered, "I've been such a fool. Such an awful fool. I believed a lie. I should have known better. I should have trusted my heart. Now I must live with the consequences," he replied with great anguish. "And so must you. I have no right to ask but please promise me one thing," Francis pleaded.

"Anything."

"Please forgive me for being so foolish and for ruining any possibility of happiness for us."

Sabina pulled away and reached up to gently caress his face as she spoke, "My darling, my love for you is so deep that I can deny you nothing. You are already forgiven."

The couple shared a kiss before Sabina turned and ran into the house. Francis stood frozen to the spot for several minutes. Finally, he made his way to the church. Francis was numb during the wedding ceremony and most of the reception. He had no idea what he was doing or saying.

By the time the reception was over, numbness had given way to fury. Rawlins had given his daughter and son-in-law a nice house on Tradd Street. The carriage drive took them to the residence but Francis did not get out with his bride. To her shock and discernment, he informed her that he would never live under the same roof with her. She had tricked him into marriage and he would never forgive or forget that fact.

Ruth was used to getting her way, so she couldn't believe it when her husband rode off to his plantation on Johns Island. Being a gentleman, Simmons honored his marriage vows by forsaking all others and paying for Ruth's bills. She made excuses for her husband's absence on social occasions, saying that it was planting or harvesting time at the plantation, he wasn't feeling well, or that it was too long a journey into Charleston.

Francis Simmons did not want excuses made on his behalf. Truth be known, he wanted to humiliate his wife. The six years they had been married seemed far longer. He was lonely and bitter. He decided to purchase property in town in the hopes he wouldn't feel so disconnected from friends and family. Francis bought a house on Legare Street but tore it down to erect a modern and lavish structure, Brick House. He spent the next three or four years making construction and decorating decisions. This kept his mind off his bad marriage, loneliness, and ennui. However, despair soon returned to his life when the house project was completed. It turned into full-blown depression when he learned Sabina had passed away. She had never married.

Her death prompted him to address his will. He left his money and possessions to family and friends. To his wife of twenty years, he left nothing. He had given her a settlement long ago to avoid dealing with her further. Francis Simmons died alone in his home.

The Brick House on Legare Street no long exists. However, horses' hooves and the sound of rumbling carriage wheels can sometimes be heard late at night. Some believe it is Francis Simmons on his way home via Sabina's. Whenever he went out, Francis always made sure to return home by way of Sabina's house. Occasionally, he would glimpse her through an open window or in the garden. He never stopped but it did bring him some comfort just to see her. Others swear the mysterious hooves and carriage sounds are Ruth Simmons on her way home. It seems that Ruth always found an excuse to pass by 14 Legare Street. Was she hoping to glimpse her estranged husband or was she just making sure he was home alone?

# THE DWARF SPIRIT

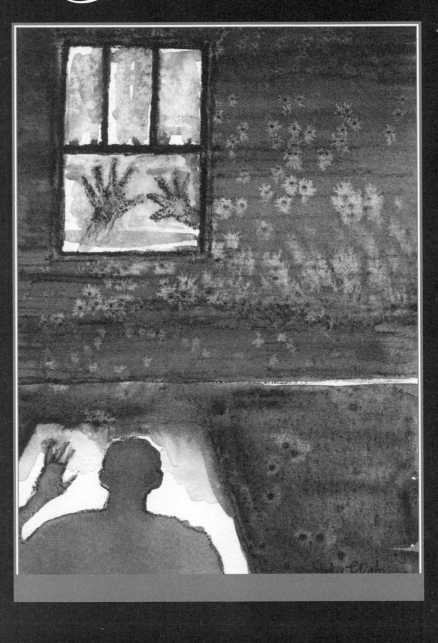

The specter's attire has been described as being pointed shoes, a cap with bells, bright-colored shirt, and stockings.

*T*he house, circa 1850s, at 411 Craven Street in Beaufort is often referred to as "The Castle." It is haunted by a Huguenot dwarf ghost named Gauche. Gauche, a professional jester, came over from France in 1562 with Jean Ribaut and other Huguenots. They established Charlesfort, which is now Parris Island, a United States Marine Base.

Accounts vary widely as to how the little man died. Some say he succumbed to disease, some say he was hanged, and some accounts claim Gauche was killed during a brawl. Author Roger Pinckney writes in *The Beaufort Chronicles* that the ghost was a Portuguese dwarf named Grenauche le Griffien, who died in 1709 during a Yemassee Indian raid.

Whatever his ethnicity or the reason for his death, the real question that begs to be asked is why he haunts a house miles away from the former Charlesfort that has no connection to him or his death. It has been surmised that Gauche or Grenauche is drawn to the dwelling because it served as a hospital, morgue, and graveyard for Federal troops who occupied it during 1861.

The original owner, Dr. Joseph Johnson, swore he saw the dwarf ghost walking outside the house. Gardeners also reported sightings. Dr. Johnson's daughter, Mrs. Lily Danner, admitted seeing the strange apparition many times when she was a child. He even attended tea parties she hosted for her dolls! The specter's attire has been described as being pointed shoes, a cap with bells, bright-colored shirt, and stockings. Just the kind of garb a jester would wear. Dr. Johnson's son also experienced ghostly encounters. He claimed the spirit was a ". . . rough little customer who always swears. . . ." Later, Lily Danner's nephew and his wife, Howard and Ruby Danner, occupied the dwelling. Guests of the Danners often reported doors opening and closing throughout the night, relocated furniture, and inexplicable bell ringing.

However, the most disturbing event has to be the handprints. Some guests say they have witnessed a fog rising out of the creek next to the house. Next, a cold breeze passed over the house, as the fog morphed into a human shape, disappearing soon thereafter. But not before leaving red handprints on the windows of the Castle!

During research on *Exploring South Carolina's Islands*, I came across a short discussion of Gauche in Nell S. Graydon's *Tales of Beaufort*. The text reveals that Gauche conversed with a houseguest late one night. This is the exchange:

"This is Gauche."

Guest: "What are you doing here?"

"I live here—in the cellar."

Guest: "Why?"

"It reminds me of my English home that I will never enter again."

Guest: "Will you let me see you?"

"No, I do not show myself to fools."

THE GENTLEMAN

GHOST AND THE
HEADLESS TORSO

What we do know is that one is known as the Gentleman Ghost and the other is the Headless Torso. The Gentleman Ghost likes to lie down beside female guests.

*T*he Carriage House Inn is situated on Charleston's historic Battery Park. The dwelling was built in 1843 by Samuel Stevens for use as a summer home. John Blacklock bought the house sixteen years later and lived there until 1870. Like much of Charleston, the house suffered damage during the Civil War. Restoration was made by its new owner, Andrew Simonds, and carried out under the direction of famous architect John Henry Devereaux. These renovations included adding a ballroom and library. Mr. Drayton Hastie and his wife, Kat, now own and operate the Carriage House Inn. It has been in his family, off and on, since 1874. Mr. Hastie's grandmother, Sara Calhoun Simonds, grew up in the house.

According to Hastie, his grandmother fell through the

ballroom skylight, but her life was saved when she landed in a chandelier. Her husband, Andrew Simonds, was founder and president of First National Bank of Charleston and the Imperial Fertilizer Company. The Simonds lived in the huge house on Battery Park for more than forty-five years. They enjoyed entertaining and frequently did so for both business and pleasure. Perhaps that is why the inn has such a highly regarded reputation.

Or maybe guests owe all that to Manager Cathy Richardson. She is responsible for all the day-to-day operations and Richardson does such a good job that some guests don't seem to want to leave. I'm talking about ghosts! This is nothing extraordinary in a place like Charleston. You are almost always in spitting distance of a ghost. In fact, several ghost walk tours are offered because there are plenty of ghosts to go around.

The story I'm about to share with you has special meaning to me because I gave my first national television interview in the Battery Carriage House Inn. I will never forget because it was July and it seemed like it was 120 degrees in Charleston—welcome to the Lowcountry. It was a hot, sunny day and I couldn't seem to get myself in a good mental place to talk spooks and specters. It seemed to me that even ghosts would lie low at this time of year. I walked into the lobby of the inn and almost immediately began to feel odd. The hair on my arms stood on end and I experienced a slight shiver. I rationally attributed this to my body's reaction to leaving the intense heat of the outdoors for the pleasant, air-conditioned interior of the inn.

I was soon approached by the producer. We exchanged brief greetings and then proceeded to Room 10, where his crew had set up the camera, audio equipment, and lights. As prearranged, the concierge had graciously accommodated us. The odd feeling I had experienced when I entered the premises heightened as I walked into this guest room. Then a sudden chill ran down my spine!

I shook all these strange feelings and listened as the producer said that he would ask me to explain the inn's ghosts and follow up with a general discussion on ghosts and hauntings. The only thing left to do before we began the interview was to make sure all systems were a go. During a short test to ensure that all recording equipment was working properly, it was discovered that the lighting was all wrong. The camera operator assured the producer that he had set it up as he had been instructed and it had looked good when he checked it earlier, but when he looked through the camera as we were about to begin, he noticed the angle was all wrong. For the second time, the camera man set up the lighting. When he finished, one of the lights that was almost directly over my head popped and went out. I nearly dove under the chair! We were delayed once again while this light was replaced. Again, the camera man swore that all the lights were new or almost new and shouldn't have burned out. We joked that maybe someone or something didn't want this interview to take place. Fortunately, there were no further problems, except for some slight audio distortion that was later discovered near the end of the interview tape.

When I finally got a chance to discuss the inn's resident ghosts, I cleared my throat (and my wandering mind) and began. "Battery Carriage House Inn actually has two ghosts. We do not know the origin of either specter. What we do know is that one is known as the Gentleman Ghost (also known as the Gentleman Caller) and the other is the Torso Ghost (also called the Headless Torso)." I looked around and bravely went on: "The well-dressed and groomed Gentleman Ghost likes to lie down beside female guests. He never disturbs them knowingly. If one wakes up and makes a frightened noise, such as a small cry or scream, he quickly exits through the nearest wall.

"The other ghost, the Torso Ghost, is not so nice. Although he has never harmed anyone, seeing this specter is a far scarier experience than witnessing the Gentleman Ghost. The Torso Ghost reveals himself less often than the Gentleman Ghost. When he does, it is a more frightening encounter, as you can well imagine. After all, this is a headless spirit! Additionally, he is clothed in a gray wool uniform and makes a deep moaning sound, as if he is in the worst pain. It is believed this is the ghost of a Confederate soldier who lost his limbs and head during an accidental munitions explosion.

"Legend has it that the Confederates were instructed to destroy caches of ammunition so as to keep it out of the hands of approaching Federals. It was believed that there was no way the Confederates could win a battle against the many troops Sherman was bringing. One casualty was the Confederate soldier whose head and limbs were blown off during their efforts. He appears in room eight at the foot of the bed or hovers over it. On rare occasions, he may touch the arm or foot of a guest."

After we'd finished taping, we packed up and got out of there. None of us talked about it afterward, but I just couldn't shake the feeling that some strange encounter had occurred. It wasn't clear enough to call it a "ghost sighting," but I still feel odd when I think about it. Certainly other visitors to the inn claim experiences more readily identifiable as sightings.

On August 8, 1992, the Torso Ghost revealed himself to a couple who later recorded the night's events in the law office of Battery Carriage House Inn owner, Drayton Hastie. Here is part of that accounting from the husband's perspective:

> . . . The bed in that room is sort of an antique bed
> that sits higher off the floor than a bed you would
> have today. So when you lie down on it you are not

at the usual level, but up a little higher. I slept on the right hand side and my wife slept on the left side. . . . I was sleeping on my side facing away from the bed looking at the wall. . . . I don't know what time it was. I don't remember. It wasn't early in the morning and it was right after I fell asleep. It was sometime in the middle of the night that I had a sensation of being watched. What I could see laying on my side with my head on the pillow was this torso of a person from the waist to the neck. I couldn't see a face. I couldn't see legs or feet but I could see its body. It was a man. It was big, not necessarily tall but broad. A strong, barrel-chested man.

He had on several layers of clothing. His overcoat was—and I distinctly remember this because I reached out and touched it—his overcoat was of very coarse material like burlap. It was very scratchy. Looking back on it, touching this thing is one of the two things that make me think it was more than just a dream. I had the real physical sensation of touching something. I remember that clearly, it wasn't just seeing it in a dream. It was a real feeling of touching.

The other thing was that this person breathed, and it was sort of raspy, like he had asthma or allergies or something. But when I reached out and touched his coat, the breath changed into the guttural growl of an animal. He moaned, or uttered some angry sound that made it clear that he didn't want me to do what I was doing. It was threatening. This thing didn't have an ax or a knife to kill me, but he was not happy that I was there. I felt like he wanted to chase me out of there. It really scared the heck out of me. It really did.

Former guests have written letters documenting personal experiences. Here are a couple of these correspondences:

In celebration of our birthday, my twin sister, Diane Smothers and I decided to treat ourselves to an overnight stay at the well-known Carriage House Inn on the Battery in Charleston, South Carolina. The date was May 19, 1992. The decor of the room was furnished in the lovely antique-style furnishings of the 1800s. Diane and I both love historic places so we were pleased with the atmosphere of the historic Carriage House. We were given room 10. Our common wall was connected to the main house.

We retired for the night about 11:00 p.m. I placed one of the antique chairs in front of the door, telling Diane that if anyone tried to enter, that the chair would be a barrier. Diane fell asleep almost immediately. I was restless and couldn't fall asleep. I was lying on the right side of the bed, facing the door. I noticed a wispy gray apparition appearing to be floating through the closed door, and through the air, entering the room. The configuration was a man with no features being visible. His height was about 5'8". No special clothes were visible; just a gray wispy shape of a slightly built man. He moved in an upright gliding motion over to my side of the bed. He lay down in a 12-inch space beside me on the bed. He placed his right arm around my shoulders. I didn't feel any pressure from his arm touching me. At no time did he speak to me. I wasn't frightened because he didn't seem threatening.

I wanted to wake Diane to let her see what was happening. I called her name several times before she woke up. She asked me what was wrong? When I tried to answer her, the figure disappeared more suddenly than he had appeared. I didn't say anything else to Diane, but relaxed and feel asleep and didn't wake till 6:00 A.M. I then asked Diane if she had seen or heard anything in the night. She said she hadn't. I related my story of the visitor during the night. She was disappointed she hadn't seen him herself.

I wished I had remained quiet and not spoken, because I feel I frightened him away. I feel that possibly his home was being disturbed by the restoration and renovation of the main house. He was looking for a place to rest and thought we might share our bed for the night.

I would love to come someday and spend another night at the Carriage House Inn to see if my "Gentleman Visitor" revisits me.

Very truly yours,

Dorothy Chmielewski

Another former guest, Andrea, shares this encounter:

My husband and I stayed at the inn in 2001 while

celebrating our fifth wedding anniversary. We were checking out the ghost tour brochures when the desk clerk asked if we knew about their ghost. We said "no" and then he checked our room number on his guest list and said, "It's okay, he's not in your room." Well, we were relieved and thought no more about hauntings at our hotel. While on our first ghost tour we were told about the pacing soldier who paces back and forth across one of the rooms at the Carriage House. He's believed to be a soldier who died on the Battery (which this house sits on). Seemed like an interesting enough story. Then, later that night or the next, I had a dream that I thought was interesting.

In the dream I was asleep next to my husband in our room at the Inn. In my dream I had on the same silk gown I was sleeping in—every detail in the dream matched reality. Then, still dreaming, I noticed a man in the room. He was dark and shadowy, with a long dark overcoat and a dark hat. He walked to the foot of our bed and grabbed my ankle. I felt it and sat straight up in bed, eyes wide open. No one but my husband and I were in the room. I didn't think too much of it because I have strange dreams all the time.

Well, the next night my husband and I took a second ghost tour. The tour guide asked if anyone was staying at the Battery Carriage House Inn. We raised our hands and she said, "Great. I am going to tell about the ghost in your hotel." I thought, "Okay, here we go with the pacing soldier again." No, she told us about the Gentleman Caller. I went cold all over. I had not heard the story of this ghost until she told it and I could not believe how closely it matched my experience.

The historic inn has eleven rooms and one suite. Continental breakfast is served and a concierge is available to assist guests. 1843 Battery Carriage House Inn Bed and Breakfast. 20 S. Battery, Charleston. 800-775-5575 or 843-727-3100. www.batterycarriage-house.com

EVIL'S CASTLE

Legend has it that if you positioned yourself at the bottom of the driveway late at night, you could see shadows "running" on the grounds.

*J*ust a few minutes from downtown Greenville lies a 1,275-acre park, which is an idyllic setting for swimming or renting a pedal boat to enjoy the large lake, picnicking, hiking, bicycling, fishing, and camping. That is, if you don't mind a few ghosts from Devil's Castle.

Devil's Castle is actually an old 36,949-square-foot edifice located on Piney Mountain, near Paris Mountain State Park. It served as the Greenville Tuberculosis Hospital from July 27, 1930, until it closed in the 1950s.

Tuberculosis, often shortened to TB and nicknamed "consumption," is a bacterial infection that can attach itself to any organ but is usually found in the lungs. Most people who are exposed to TB never develop symptoms and the bacteria can live in an inactive form in the body. However, if the immune system weakens, the bacteria can activate and result in death.

Because the bacteria are transmitted through the air, the disease can be highly communicable. However, it is very rare to catch TB simply by passing an infected person on the street. To be at risk, you must be exposed to the organisms constantly, by living or working in close quarters with someone who has the active disease. This is why TB sanitariums or hospitals were established. Family could come visit without risk but it was not advisable to live with infected persons. This was a frightening, widespread disease until the 1950s when antibiotics were developed that fought TB.

For a while, the hospital at 220 Beverly Road also accommodated the criminally insane. And then the facility sat abandoned for many years until it became a work release center for prisoners from 1974 to 1997. Ghostly sightings and other unexplainable experiences have occurred over the years.

Legend has it that if you positioned yourself at the bottom of the driveway late at night, you could see shadows "running" on the grounds. Also, the sound of running footsteps could be heard inside the old dwelling even when no one could be seen running. There have also been unexplainable flickering lights and clanking noises.

Who is responsible for these sounds and sights? Is it the spirits of TB patients who are finally free? Or is it the spirits of the criminally insane who once were impounded here? Perhaps it is the ghosts of former prisoners?

Devil's Castle had deteriorated into a state of disrepair and was scheduled to be destroyed in late 1999 but received a reprieve from the wrecking ball while state and county officials explored the possibility of making it a veterans' hospital.

The structure suffered significant damage in November 2002 when a fire occurred, but visitors to the area and Paris Mountain State Park still report bizarre experiences that leave them with more memories than they anticipated. Maybe the spirits of Devil's Castle relocated when their dwelling burned or perhaps they just needed more room to roam. . . .

Take SC 253 six miles north of Greenville and follow the signs for Paris Mountain State Park. 2401 State Park Road, Greenville. 864-244-5565. www.wildernet.com. The park is maintained by the South Carolina Department of Parks and Tourism.

DUPRE HOUSE

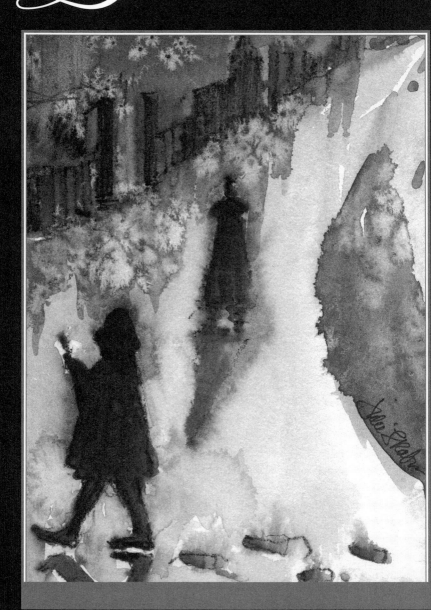

GHOSTS

Previous owners and guests have heard a small child crying out for its mother, witnessed wisps of smoke, smelled smoke, glimpsed small footprints, seen the child looking for its mother, and seen a young woman wearing a long dress.

Georgetown, situated on the Atlantic Ocean where the Waccamaw, Black, Sampit, and Pee Dee Rivers meet to form Winyah Bay, is the third oldest port in the state. It began as a Spanish settlement in 1526, but was later abandoned because of a fever epidemic. The English settled here in 1700, and the first land grant was issued in 1705 to John Perry by the Lords Proprietors. The first parish, Prince George, Winyah, was granted in 1722 to Baptist minister Elisha Screven, but it was five more years before this parish officially became Georgetown, so named after England's King George II.

In 1734, Screven divided the 275 acres into lots. The preacher envisioned seven streets perpendicular to the Sampit River and five streets running parallel to it. Each block would contain 230 lots. The DuPre House is situated on Lot 53. The dwelling has had many owners through the years, including Paul Trapier, who earned the nickname "King of Georgetown" because he owned so much property and played such a prominent role in the town's development. The house is named after the DuPres, a French Huguenot family that once owned the residence.

The circa 1790 house has been renovated many times over the years and it was made into a bed and breakfast inn many years ago and is a popular choice for vacationers because of its ideal location in Georgetown's Historic District. Another reason guests enjoy staying in this pre-Revolutionary War house is that it is skillfully decorated throughout with art and antiques.

All five guestrooms have four-poster beds and private bathrooms. Guests may choose to stay in rooms with a fireplace, Jacuzzi tub, or private verandah. All guests may enjoy the lush gardens, swimming pool, hot tub, and rocking chairs. A couple of Pawleys Island hammocks have been carefully placed between hundred-year-old oak trees. A full breakfast is served daily and complimentary beverages are available in the late afternoon.

Guests may also have a ghostly encounter—at no extra cost! Previous owners and guests have heard a small child crying out for its mother, witnessed wisps of smoke, smelled smoke, glimpsed small footprints, seen the child who was looking for its mother, and seen a young woman wearing a long dress. None of the events could ever be rationalized so the conclusion was made that the residence must be haunted.

Guests staying in the third-floor front bedroom are most likely to have some kind of ghostly experience. A former owner once felt a hand on his shoulder as he made up the bed in that room. This spooked him because he was not a believer in ghosts and yet there was no other logical explanation. No one else was in the room and there was no mistaking the fact that someone had placed a firm hand on his shoulder. He left the room for a few minutes to get a grip on himself.

During this time he talked himself into believing he had imagined what had happened. The innkeeper returned to finish making up the bed and tidying the room. As soon as he bent down to finish making up the bed, he felt the same firm hand on his shoulder. He couldn't talk himself out of the experience this time!

The house was once owned by Mrs. Easterling. The widow inherited her husband's highly profitable ice business. The ice house was across the street from the DuPre House. Shortly after his death, the widow had the upper level of the business renovated into an apartment. Mrs. Easterling and her child moved out of DuPre House and into the ice house apartment. She held onto the house but just couldn't bear to live in it any longer.

Early one evening, Mrs. Easterling called to the child to come inside for supper. The child, who had been playing on the front steps, raced inside. One of the toys left behind on the wooden steps was a box that had been made into a house. Holes had been cut in the small box to serve as windows and a tiny candle had been placed inside to illuminate the play house.

The candle caused a fire. Luckily, Mrs. Easterling awoke and got her child outside to safety. Unfortunately, she ran back in the burning building to retrieve some valuables. The roof fell in on her and she died in the fire. Many believe that it must be the orphaned child and Mrs. Easterling that haunt the DuPre House where they were once so happy.

The DuPre House Bed and Breakfast Inn is in the Georgetown Historic District, one block from the waterfront. 921 Prince Street. 843-546-0298 or 877-519-9499. www.duprehouse.com.

$\mathcal{L}$OWCOUNTRY

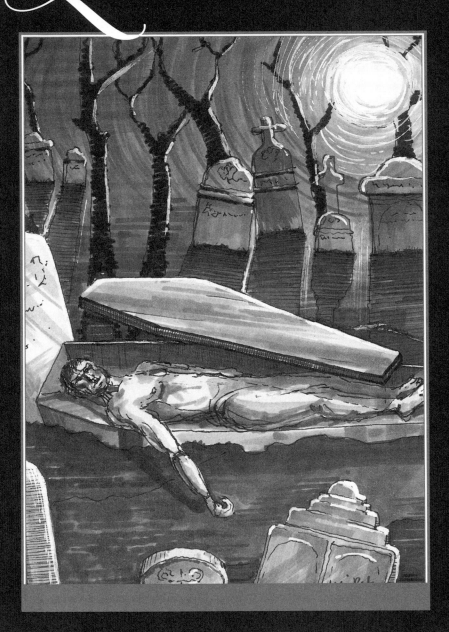

Upon his death, his body parts were used by other root doctors for special conjuring.

This story centers around black magic, conjurors, evil spells, witch doctors, incantations, sorcery, and root doctoring. Before I get to the story about the infamous Dr. Buzzard, I first need to explain a few things. Gullahs are descendants of West African slaves who worked on area plantations. After slavery ended, they remained in the Lowcountry and became fishermen, hunters, and farmers. Their language is a Creole blend of European and African languages. The Gullahs believe strongly in signs and rituals and have passed these beliefs and traditions to their kin.

BAD OMENS OR TABOOS

- Never try on someone else's hat or let someone wear your hat.
- Never shake hands. It will put a curse on both persons.
- Never let someone comb your hair.
- Stomping your left foot is bad luck; stomping the right foot

is good luck, and you should wish for something after doing so.

- If your right hand itches, it means you will receive a letter; if your left hand itches, it means you will receive money. If your nose itches, someone will soon be visiting.
- If a rooster crows at night, someone you know will die.

GOOD OMENS

- If you see a red bird on your doorstep, count to nine and money will follow.
- "Hoppin' John," blackeyed peas, rice, and ham boiled together and eaten on New Year's Day will bring a prosperous year.
- When you awaken on the first day of the month and say "rabbit" before you get out of bed, it will be a good month.
- Wishes made to a new moon will come true, as will dreams beneath a new quilt.

It is difficult to learn about Gullahs because their language is hard to understand, and they will only share so much information with outsiders. I did come across some insightful information in *Folk-Lore of the Sea Island, South Carolina*. Here are some Gullah sayings and beliefs:

DREAM

"Dream 'bout snames, have somet'in' to fight, some kin' tem'-tation."

WEATHER SIGNS

"Ef a cat wash her face, it goin' to rain."

LUCK

"De firs' time you sleep in a strange house, make a wish, an' it comes true."

HEALTH

For general ailments, a dime with a hole in it is tied around the ankle. For a headache, a string is tied around the head.

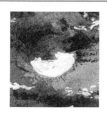 Penn Center & York W. Bailey Museum details the history of Penn Center and of the Gullah culture. Originally used as a school, it was established in 1862 for freed island slaves by Laura Towne, an abolitionist and Unitarian. It later served as a center of reform. Cultural programs and lectures are given here, and dorm rooms and cottages are available. Penn Center Heritage Days Celebration is held every November. Additionally, the center can provide specific information on the Beaufort area and St. Helena Island Gullah tours offered by locals. St. Helena is twelve miles from Beaufort. (843) 838-8560. www.penncenter.com.

For more information on St. Helena Island, you may be interested in reading *Exploring South Carolina's Islands* (Terrance Zepke, Pineapple Press). For more information on the Gullahs and their beliefs, *Blue Roots* (Roger Pinckney, Llewellyn Publications) is an excellent resource.

According to Nell Graydon in *Tales of Edisto*, 1955, some aspects of African voodoo were still practiced on the island at that time, though many of the practices had disappeared with each new generation. Some of the remaining customs and beliefs included superstitions, especially concerning the dead. The Gullahs painted their doors and shutters a bright blue to keep out evil spirits. They claimed these "sparits" assumed many forms, including dogs, goats, and other animals, when they rose from their graves after midnight. The Gullahs also believed that some old women had the power to make love charms and cast spells that cause sickness or even death. Dried frogs and snakes and black cats were used to brew concoctions for various purposes.

Graydon demonstrates these beliefs by citing some examples, including a personal experience. She once had a laundress named Toria who took ill. They tried various treatments but nothing worked. She offered to take Toria to a doctor in Charleston but the woman refused. "T'ain't no use, Missus," she said sadly. "I gwine see death. Beula, 'e done hab ole Riah f'row spell puntop me. Just yestiddy top do'step uh fin' dried toad. T'ain't no use." (Loosely translated: Toria told Graydon that it was no use going to see a doctor because Beulah had gotten Mariah to cast a spell on her [Toria]. Her proof was that she had found a dried toad at the top of her steps yesterday.)

Having heard of Mariah and her reputation for conjuring charms, Graydon went to the woman's cabin to ask her to leave Toria alone. She also gave her a bribe of two bags of tobacco and several small pieces of silver. Mariah grinned and snatched the items, promising "Fuh sutt'n, Missus, Riah help Toria. Tell she attuh w'ile she be well. Riah sus so." The message was delivered to Toria and sure enough, the woman was soon well.

When Toria's husband, Bi'man, complained of chest pains, Toria begged Graydon to intercede again. A woman named Beulah had fallen in love with Bi'man, but he had resisted her advances. The couple believed Beulah had gotten Mariah to cast a spell. Once more, Graydon rode down the sand road to Riah's cabin and took bribes—tobacco and groceries. The purpose of the visit had not yet been explained, but the woman seemed to know already. After examining the goods, she pulled a corncob doll, which looked like a man, from an old chest. A string was wrapped tightly around the doll's chest and as the woman unwound the cord that smelled strongly of kerosene, she told Graydon to take the doll to Toria and to tell her to keep it and no sparits would ever harm her family. Although Nell Graydon had a hard time imagining how unraveling a string from a doll could cure someone, Bi'man's pains stopped almost immediately.

Root doctoring is just another form of conjuring, and here's a story about the most renowned root doctor in South Carolina. It is popularly believed that Dr. Buzzard, aka Stephaney Robinson, learned this skill from his father, who was supposedly smuggled from Africa aboard an illegal slave ship. Dr. Buzzard, however, claims to have gotten his mantle (power) from a mockingbird. Regardless of the origin, folks around St. Helena Island believed he possessed a powerful mantle.

His appearance certainly lent credibility to his claims. The dark man wore loose, black clothing and thick, purple eyeglasses. The dark shades guaranteed that no one could look into his eyes. He concocted all kinds of potions and often used animals in his rituals, such as cats and snakes.

You may wonder who sought out this witch doctor and for what purpose? Some were trying to reconnect with deceased relatives. Others, who were in trouble with the law, were seeking retribution. Still others were defendants who enlisted his aid to get a favorable outcome in their court cases.

Dr. Buzzard's home, Oaks Plantation, was on the southwest tip of St. Helena Island. Once a week he made a trip inland to the Frogmore Post Office to check his post office box. Every week there were dozens of letters from across the state and several neighboring states, as well. Most contained cash, checks, or money orders. The shrewd man pocketed the cash but threw away the payments that required his signature. Root doctoring was illegal because it was practicing medicine without a license. The witch doctor wasn't about to get caught in a trap.

People came from near and far wanting Dr. Buzzard to work his magic. His audience increased tenfold as more and more incredible stories circulated. One involved a Gullah fishing party that drowned. The men had set out in two boats but had met with so much success that the second boat was loaded down with fish and the men all piled into the smaller boat. On the return trip, there was a terrible storm and the men drowned. Two days later, the boat full of fish arrived at shore with a big buzzard resting atop of them! The Gullahs took it as a sign—this was Dr. Buzzard's doing, they were sure of it.

It was even rumored that the root doctor sent his boat and buzzards to bring a potential client to him. One buzzard steered and the others rowed with their wings. If the person wasn't sincere, the buzzards would know and drown him. There were many other stories. Who knows which ones, if any, are true or partially true.

One undisputed tale is about a flock of buzzards that showed up one day and made their home at the top of Beaufort's city water tower. The Beaufort County Courthouse was located in front of the water tower. When Dr. Buzzard made a court appearance on behalf of a client, the buzzards left their perch atop the tower and flew around the courthouse several times. The Gullahs took this as a sure sign that Dr. Buzzard's mantle was working perfectly.

To sway the outcome of a trial or court proceeding, Gullah defendants sometimes hired root doctors to come into court and work their magic, or at least send along a strong root or powder concoction. Dr. Buzzard was inarguably the best root doctor, and if his high fees could be paid, he would come to court and speak in tongues, give the evil eye to adversaries, chew on a root, or whatever he deemed most effective. On these occasions, court proceedings were turned topsy turvy. Imagine the scene: the huge, soaring buzzards circling overhead outside the courthouse, the ominous black clothing and thick purple eyeglasses worn by the notorious Dr. Buzzard, and his entourage of admirers and curiosity seekers. How intimidating this all must have been to witnesses, jurors, and opposing counsel! I imagine that even the judge must have been taken aback.

One of the few people not overwhelmed or bullied by these tactics was the new sheriff, J. E. McTeer. Soon after he won the 1926 election, the law enforcement officer witnessed some remarkable things, such as people getting sick and dying for no apparent reason and witnesses suffering seizures in the middle of testifying. McTeer was no stranger to this stuff. He knew it was the work of conjurors. His grandfather was a rice planter who had had several slaves who practiced black magic. His grandmother was a medium for the spirit world and McTeer recalled one séance that he had witnessed in his grandparent's home when he was just a boy. He remembered it so well because the table moved and shook when his grandmother placed her arms and hands on top of it.

The sheriff also believed he had inherited some of his grandmother's gift. McTeer felt strongly that the only way to stop the rampant black magic was to stop Dr. Buzzard. He devised a plan but before it could be carried out, World War II came to the

Lowcountry. McTeer was responsible for overseeing beach patrols and his mind was far from Dr. Buzzard until the military kept rejecting the draftees from St. Helena Island.

The draft board sent many Gullah men to Fort Jackson, but the base sent most of the men back home, citing poor health. The military physicians had named the condition "hippity-hoppity heart syndrome." It was no freak coincidence that these men shared the same ailments, diarrhea and heart palpitations. McTeer was so sure of this he sent a letter to the War Department outlining his beliefs and the reason for them. The government didn't hold much stock in McTeer's claims until a busload of St. Helena Island recruits became critically ill on their way to Fort Jackson. One man died before reaching the hospital.

An investigation revealed that these men had ingested potions they had purchased for $50 apiece that were guaranteed to make them slightly sick and get them released from military duty. Despite their initial cooperation, none of the young men dared testify against a mighty root doctor, let alone the greatest root doctor, Dr. Buzzard. McTeer, with a great deal of persuasion, managed to obtain a small bottle of this potion from one of the sick men. Autopsy results showed that the deceased had ingested a double dose of the potion to be certain he failed his physical and avoided military service. The tests also proved the potion was a mixture of oleander leaves (digitalis), rubbing alcohol, moth balls, and lead. No wonder the young men suffered wild heart palpitations!

J.E. McTeer was sure he had Dr. Buzzard for this crime. However, the pharmacy records proved it was another root doctor, Dr. Bug, who purchased the arsenic and created the lethal tonics. Strangely, Dr. Bug didn't even deny his role in the deception. He was found guilty and forced to pay a hefty fine. Soon thereafter, Dr. Bug took to his bed and died within the year.

 Root doctors were tolerated during the days of slavery because traditional treatments and cures were poor, to say the least. Confederate army surgeon, Francis Porcher, asked root doctors and Indians for herbal remedies when supply lines were damaged during the Civil War. With the advances of modern medicine, the herbal remedies promised by root doctors are frowned upon. There are stores that carry such products but the labels are carefully marked "may" or "alleged" rather than guaranteeing success. It's interesting that the root may or may not contain herbs. The root may be a charm or mojo that is chewed, worn, or buried, depending on the root doctor's instructions. Some "classic" roots include "Follow Me" (love charm), "Money Root" (money charm)," "John the Conqueror" (power charm), and "Blue Root" (mostly used to cause illness).

Just as important as the ingredients are the ritual performed by the root doctor while creating the charm and the proper use of the charm. The words spoken and actions taken by the root doctor while making the charm are never revealed. However, we do know some of the popular ingredients found in them. Goofer dust is graveyard dirt gathered just before midnight from the grave of a righteous Christian if the root will be used for a good charm, or just after midnight from the grave of a lost soul for bad charms. Goofer originated from the African word, *kuwfa*, meaning "dead person." It's important to note that the Gullahs believe in both conjuration and Christianity.

Various herbs, sulphur, salt, candle wax, incense, asafedita, and gunpowder may be used in good luck charms, while crow feathers, salamander feet, and animal parts are used in bad luck charms.

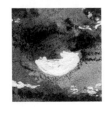There is a legend that one of the many times that Dr. Buzzard was arrested or brought in for questioning to the sheriff who had defeated McTeer, he told his captors that he had absolute proof that he was a bona fide witch doctor. He was no charlatan, he assured them. To prove his point, he asked that they lock him in a coffin and he promised them he could escape. This they had to see, the jailers told him. A coffin was brought to the building and Dr. Buzzard got into it. As he lay down, he told them he would be out by the time they finished their midday meal.

The coffin was closed and chains were wrapped around it. The locks were secured and the men laughingly proceeded across the street to eat lunch. When they returned, they found the chains and locks lying on the floor near the coffin. The coffin was opened and a black cat jumped out!

Sheriff McTeer never gave up his campaign to stop Dr. Buzzard. He nearly had the witch doctor when a burglary suspect was apprehended with a root and bag of white powder. The suspect refused to answer his questions until McTeer put on purple eyeglasses that closely resembled those worn by Dr. Buzzard. The suspect broke down and confessed everything. Dr. Buzzard had sold him the root to make him invisible and the white powder was to prevent his capture.

Despite this knowledge, the case never made it to court. As soon as the witness saw Dr. Buzzard enter the interrogation room, he started shaking, fell to the floor, and began rolling around violently. Sheriff McTeer knew the poor man would never be able to testify against the root doctor and dismissed the charges against Dr. Buzzard. He issued a warning that if the witch doctor didn't stop, he would eventually bring him to justice.

The great root doctor was not accustomed to being threatened. In fact, it made him so mad that he set out to ruin the sheriff. The spiritual warfare came to a halt after Dr. Buzzard's son was killed in a car crash. The conjuror believed the wreck was McTeer's doing and went to see his adversary. The root doctor told the sheriff that he respected his mantle and would leave him alone if McTeer would do the same. The law man agreed, so long as Buzzard quit practicing sorcery. Dr. Buzzard thought about this for several seconds before slowly nodding his head in agreement.

Dr. Buzzard was later caught root doctoring. He hired a white lawyer to defend him, but was found guilty and ordered to pay a fine. He died a few months later of stomach cancer.

At the next election, a former highway patrolman challenged McTeer. The candidate put on an aggressive campaign and there was mud-slinging on both sides. The race was so tight that a TV debate was scheduled. Both sides had a great deal riding on the outcome of this debate. McTeer, being the incumbent, was allowed to go first. He spoke at length about his commitment to the public, his longstanding, impressive record, and deep ties to the community. When it came time for the opponent to make his speech, all the TVs in the area succumbed to static interference.

Nonetheless, the challenger won by a narrow margin. McTeer retired and the new sheriff took office. His term was tumultuous, ending with the assault of a grand jury foreman, who just happened to be a retired brigadier general. The sheriff fled the courtroom, locked himself in his house, and threatened suicide. Officials managed to get him out of the house and into counseling. Many locals believed this was the work of J. E. McTeer, but he made no such claim.

Although the former sheriff wrote a book, *Fifty Years as a Lowcountry Witch Doctor*, he refused to comment on the subject of root doctoring. When he died in 1976, his son became the only white root doctor in Beaufort County. Likewise Dr. Buzzard's powers extended to his son, Buzzy, who practiced root doctoring until his death in 1997.

The whereabouts of Dr. Buzzard's grave remain a secret. There is an unmarked gravesite in a Baptist church cemetery on St. Helena Island that a few believe belongs to Dr. Buzzard. However, some swear he never was buried and that upon his death, his body parts were used by other root doctors for special conjuring.

CONDUCTING A

GHOST HUNT

I've been asked by many folks, how do you conduct a ghost hunt? First, you should understand some basic "ghost" terminology. These definitions come from the South Carolina Paranormal Research Investigation Group.

Apparition: Manifestation of a spirit visible to the eye.

Cold Spot: Phenomena in which part of a haunted area has a significantly lower room temperature.

EVP (Electronic Voice Phenomenon): The occurrence of phantom voices on tape, which some believe allows communication with the deceased. The sounds are thought to be the voices of spirits. These sounds aren't normally heard by the human ear, but can sometimes be picked up by recording devices. (Weird, drawn-out voices—loud screaming or faint voices, growls, squeals, groans, etc.)

Malevolent Spirit: A spirit exhibiting destructive behavior or harmful intentions.

Orb: Anomalous or unexplained energy caught on film usually in association with a haunting, high EMF readings, and cold spots. They range through a variety of sizes and colors, the most common being white. They are usually spherical.

Paranormal: Any event or object that defies scientific explanation or knowledge.

Poltergeist: A haunting that involves noisy spirits and no visible manifestations.

Portal haunting: A doorway or portal that provides access for spirits to enter our world from another dimension. A very common doorway is a cemetery or a graveyard.

Psycho Kinetic Activity: The movement of objects by spirits and the movement of objects caused by living persons with extreme emotions.

Reciprocal Apparition: This is a rare occurrence when both the agent (the spirit visitor) and the percipient (the visited person) see each other.

Residual Haunting: When a spirit becomes trapped in a terrible emotional loop, such as a traumatic event, that repeats itself. The apparition does not interact with you.

Spirit: Soul, essence, or spirit of a deceased person. Earthbound spirits are those who have not passed over. They are trapped between worlds.

Spirits: The electromagnetic identity (orbs, mist, vortexes, or shadows) of a former living person who has returned to their original home location to visit relatives or effect unfulfilled wishes.

Vortex: Energy that takes the shape of a tube in a photograph. It may vary in color and shape. It may appear to be a camera strap in the photo. We have seen various colors in vortex photos. One theory is that they are made up of several orbs. It may be in connection with a portal or doorway. Geomagnetic energy anomaly and not spirits can cause vortex photos. There is often a high EMF reading when an orb is present.

Next, there are some tips and techniques you should know.

PHOTOGRAPHS

For taking photographs, higher speed films, such as 400 and 800, work best. Be sure to have a fresh battery in the camera and at least one spare battery with you. Make sure your camera is in good working condition and that the lens is clean. Look around and familiarize yourself with any lights or reflective surfaces that may interfere with your picture taking. You don't want to mistake a light or reflection for an orb! The same holds true for long hair, loose clothing, or the camera strap. These may end up in front of the lens, giving the mistaken impression of a vortex.

Be careful that you don't take photos at the exact same time as someone else. The simultaneous flash may be mistaken for a ghostly image. Don't be economical with the film. Take lots of photos and remember that you don't have to see a ghost for evidence of one to appear on film or tape. Be sure that wherever you take your film for processing you tell the lab that you want all rolls developed. You don't want the technician making decisions on your behalf.

If you'll be using a digital camera or camcorder, make sure it can record in low light. Ideally, you'll have both a camera and camcorder to record events.

Expert ghost hunters advise asking the ghost if you can take its picture, assuming you see a ghostly apparition, of course.

Just a reminder, there are three ways that ghosts show up in photos: as mist (foglike discoloration), vortexes (crescent-shaped pale areas that are usually white), and orbs (round pale areas resembling globes or balls of light). Orbs are most common.

EQUIPMENT

Photographic equipment has already been discussed. Also, each of you should have a good flashlight with fresh batteries. A pen or pocket-size flashlight will probably not provide enough light. You may want to bring a tape recorder with a microphone and fresh batteries. Additionally, you may wish to bring along a notepad and pencil to sketch what you see. A cheap set of walkie talkies may come in handy.

Serious sleuths take along a digital or electronic thermometer or thermal scanner to detect cold spots. A motion detector senses movement by unseen objects or forces. An EMF detector reads an area's electromagnetic fields.

ATTITUDE

Be prepared and sharp. If you are serious about your investigation, you will avoid alcoholic beverages before or during the study so as to have your wits about you. Also, don't talk, smoke, or wear cologne/perfume because spirits often emit sounds and scents to get attention.

Do your homework. Make sure you know what it is you're

investigating. Check out the place in advance. This will keep you from driving in circles trying to find a turn off or parking spot. Be sure you're not trespassing. Trespassers run the risk of getting arrested or worse. Before setting out, make sure you have all the equipment you need.

MISCELLANEOUS

Take someone with you. Always follow the buddy system. Watch where you're stepping so that you don't trip over a tree root or twist an ankle stepping in a hole. Wear sneakers or some other type of sturdy shoe. Remember, the best time for ghost sightings is typically late at night and into the wee hours of the morning.

Lastly, you may wish to do some additional research or join an amateur "ghost sleuthing" group. Below are some resources that may be helpful. Please note that these organizations may provide useful information to those interested in learning more about this subject, but neither the author nor publisher endorses them or the links that may be offered on their websites.

You may also be interested to know that Charleston, Georgetown, and Beaufort offer good ghost walks or tours. Just ask at the local visitor's center for more information.

Best of luck!

RESOURCES

American Ghost Society
www.praiseghosts.com/ags.htm

American Society for Paranormal Research and Investigation
http://www.angelfire.com/sc3/aspri/aspri.html

Lowcountry Paranormal Investigators
http://www.geocities.com/yankybelle/paranormal.htm

The International Ghost Hunters Society
www.ghostweb.com

The ShadowLands
www.theshadowlands.net

South Carolina Paranormal Research Investigation Group
www.ghosthuntersinc.com/ghostgroups.htm
www.angelfire.com/ct2/PDIG/PSIG.html

Ghosts and Legends TheatreBarefoot Landing, North Myrtle Beach. "Come meet the locals" in this live action show where ghosts tell their own stories as the theatre comes to life all around you. Historical, educational, and chilling tales unfold in a classic Southern plantation parlor—once you pass through its secret panel entrance. Meet the famous pirate Blackbeard, survive a category-four hurricane, and more. Enjoy this genuinely haunting South Carolina experience and become a part of the Southern storytelling tradition.

Ghosts and Legends Theatre is open all year, with shows performed daily every half hour. 843-361-2700 www.GhostShows.com

INDEX

If you enjoyed reading this book, here are some other books from Pineapple Press on related topics. For a complete catalog, write to Pineapple Press, P.O. Box 3889, Sarasota, FL 34230 or call 1-800-PINEAPL (746-3275). Or visit our website at www.pineapplepress.com.

Exploring South Carolina's Islands by Terrance Zepke. A complete guide for vacationers, day-trippers, armchair travelers, and people looking to relocate to this charming area. What to see and do, where to stay and eat on South Carolina's fabled islands, with over 70 photos. ISBN 1-56164-259-2 (pb)

Ghosts of St. Augustine by Dave Lapham. The unique and often turbulent history of America's oldest city is told in twenty-four spooky stories that cover four hundred years' worth of ghosts. ISBN 1-56164-123-5 (pb)

Ghosts of the Carolina Coasts by Terrance Zepke. Taken from real-life occurrences and Carolina Lowcountry lore, these thirty-two spine-tingling ghost stories take place in prominent historic structures of the region. ISBN 1-56164-175-8 (pb)

Haunt Hunter's Guide to Florida by Joyce Elson Moore. Discover the general history and "haunt" history of numerous sites around the state where ghosts reside. ISBN 1-56164-150-2 (pb)

Haunted Lighthouses and How to Find Them by George Steitz. The producer of the popular TV series *Haunted Lighthouses* takes you on a tour of America's most enchanting and mysterious lighthouses. ISBN 1-56164-268-1 (pb)

Haunting Sunshine by Jack Powell. Take a wild ride though the shadows of the Sunshine State in this collection of deliciously creepy stories of ghosts in the theatres, churches, and historic places of Florida. ISBN 1-56164-220-7 (pb)

Lighthouses of the Carolinas by Terrance Zepke. Eighteen lighthouses aid mariners traveling the coasts of North and South Carolina. Here is the story of each, from origin to current status, along with visiting information and photographs. Newly revised to include up-to-date information on the long-awaited and much-debated Cape Hatteras Lighthouse move, plus websites for area visitors' centers and tourist bureaus. ISBN 1-56164-148-0 (pb)

Oldest Ghosts by Karen Harvey. In St. Augustine (the oldest settlement in the New World), the ghost apparitions are as intriguing as the city's history. ISBN 1-56164-222-3 (pb)

The Best Ghost Tales of North Carolina by Terrance Zepke. The actors of North Carolina's past linger among the living in this thrilling collection of ghost tales. Experience the chilling encounters told by the winners of the North Carolina "Ghost Watch" contest. Use Zepke's tips to conduct your own ghost hunt. ISBN 1-56164-233-9 (pb)